the new ze

ITALIAN

cookbook

the new zealand
ITALIAN
cookbook

shirley bradstock

GODWIT

First published 1996 by

Godwit Publishing Ltd
15 Rawene Road, P.O. Box 34-683
Birkenhead, Auckland, New Zealand

ISBN 0 908877 96 X

Text and cover design by Sarah Maxey
Cover illustration by Daniel Pudles
Production by Kate Greenaway
Printed by GP Print, Wellington

Contents

Abbreviations and measurements

Abbreviations

ml	millilitre
g	gram
kg	kilogram
cm	centimetre
mm	millimetre
°C	degrees Celsius

Measurements

New Zealand standard metric kitchen measures have been used for all the recipes. All measures should be level.

1 cup holds 250 ml
1 tablespoon holds 15 ml
1 dessertspoon holds 10 ml
1 teaspoon holds 5 ml

(The Australian metric tablespoon holds 20 ml or 4 teaspoons.)

Equivalents

(To the nearest 5 grams)

grams	ounces
30	1
55	2
85	3
100	$3\frac{1}{2}$
115	4
140	5
170	6
200	7
225	8
280	10
340	12
390	14
455	16 (one pound)

Oven temperatures

(Conversions are approximate)

	°C	°F
	100	200
	110	225
very cool	120	250
	140	275
	150	300
	160	325
cool		
	180	350
	190	375
moderate		
	200	400
	220	425
	230	450
hot		
	250	475
	260	500
very hot		

Note: All servings are for 4–6 people unless specified otherwise.

Introduction

Italian cooking is not just pizza, pasta and incredibly rich desserts, although all these are part of this endlessly varied and beautifully simple cuisine. Said to be one of the oldest in Europe, Italian cuisine was originally influenced by Greek traditions, further developed in ancient Rome and ultimately fine-tuned into the Italian style we know today.

There are several reasons why Italian food is so popular in New Zealand. First, New Zealand ingredients lend themselves particularly well to the Italian way of cooking. Second, Italian food is among the longer-established cuisines in this country — every New Zealand city worth its salt has had Italian restaurants for many years. And third, because we Kiwis travel a lot these days and are exposed to new and interesting foods, our tastes have become wider and more sophisticated.

This book concentrates on treating our New Zealand ingredients in an Italian way. Throughout I try to emphasise how to get the best from food by bringing out the intrinsic flavours, not overpowering them with sauces or dominating herbs and spices, and definitely not overcooking them.

The essence of Italian cooking is fresh food prepared simply. Our temperate New Zealand climate gives us a long growing season, so we are lucky enough to have seasonal foods available for more of each year. Some foods used in Italian cooking, such as seafood and mushrooms, are plentiful year round here because we have large fishing and horticulture industries, and well-stocked shops to bring their products to the public.

Then, of course, there is our wonderful dairy produce. Although only a few local cheese factories are making classic Italian cheeses at present, this situation is rapidly changing for the better. No other country has finer cream and butter — and now

Introduction

we are even starting to produce top quality olives and olive oils. Many of these local products compare well with the authentic products, but some are not as good. True Italian parmesan, for example, is still much better than the local product, and worth the extra cost. With Kiwi ingenuity, we can expect many further exciting developments of a unique 'hybrid' New Zealand/Italian cuisine. Might we be seeing in the future whitebait frittata, lamb and kumara pizza, puha tortellini?

Not only do we now have a whole range of Italian-style foods made right here in New Zealand, but importers are providing us with all sorts of Italian goods, from pastas to fine wines. The Italians set a very high standard for their exports, which means we are often able to get some of the very best Italy has to offer.

The pasta chapter is a large one since there are so many things you can do with pasta. Dried pasta is perfectly acceptable for most of these recipes but fresh pasta is easy to make and infinitely versatile. Sheets of fresh pasta are used for lasagne or cut into ribbons of various sizes to serve with sauces. Fresh pasta can also be cut into shapes that are filled to make ravioli, cappelletti or tortellini. And all of these can be made in different colours, depending on the dough you use.

Italian soups, side dishes, vegetables and rice dishes are so interesting and varied that I wish I could have included many more. They all show just how well suited local ingredients are to the Italian way of cooking.

Pizza makes a great family meal for busy Kiwis: it's easy, quick, and versatile and nutritious — and there's almost no cleaning up at the end. I have also covered the making of pizza bread (called focaccia or schiacciata) as well as pizza bases and a number of topping suggestions. I introduce, too, the concept of sweet pizzas.

Although Italians don't have a fancy dessert every day, they make some delicious desserts. I have provided a range from simple cool granitas to the extremely rich zuppa inglese. I hope you find plenty here to tempt you. *Buon appetito*!

Glossary

Al dente. A term meaning 'firm to the bite' which is used to describe the texture of cooked pasta and rice. It means a firm texture – not raw, but not overcooked.

Anchovies. Small silvery fish found in coastal waters. They are available filleted and packed in oil, or whole packed in salt. Anchovies canned in oil are most widely available here. They are quite easy to use and keep well in the refrigerator once opened.

Arborio rice. A short-grained rice which is particularly suitable for risottos as it absorbs so much of the stock in which it is cooked. You may need to buy arborio rice from delis specialising in Italian goods, although it is now often available in supermarkets. The best substitute for arborio is long-grained or even extra-long-grained rice.

Artichokes. The flowerhead of a thistle-like plant (*Cynara scolymus*), the heart of which is the main part eaten. Although frequently used in Italian cooking, artichokes are often impossible to buy fresh in the shops. They are, however, very hardy and easy to grow, as well as being decorative in the garden, so you might consider growing a few from seed or suckers. One plant should produce 8–10 flowerheads, which need to be picked before the bracts or scales start to turn brownish, a sign they are about to flower. For many recipes you can use marinated or tinned artichokes, which are readily available from delis and better supermarkets.

Balsamic vinegar. A deep tawny-red vinegar made in the northern region of Italy from Trebbiano grapes and aged in oak barrels for anywhere from 3 to 50 years. The flavour is rich and mellow and well worth the extra cost.

Basil. A herb (*Ocimum basilicum*) used fresh in pesto, sauces and salads. Dried basil may be used in sauces and soups but never for pesto. Fresh basil may be puréed and frozen for that wonderful summery taste in winter.

Biscotti. Sweet biscuits (cookies) which are baked twice to make them very dry. They keep very well for a long time and are served with coffee or wine as dunkers.

Bocconcini. Small balls of mozzarella each weighing about 100 g. They are stored in their own whey or a light brine and are eaten fresh. They are sometimes sold in the dairy section of the grocery store or in delicatessens specialising in Italian products.

Brodo. Italian broth or stock which is quite lightly flavoured and usually made from meat rather than bones.

Bruschetta. The Umbrian name for a thick slice of bread toasted and brushed with extra virgin olive oil and often rubbed with garlic after toasting. In Tuscany the same thing is called fettunta.

Cappelletti. Small square or circles of pasta that are filled and folded in half and then pinched together around the finger to form a little hat shape. This is the Romagna name for tortellini.

Capers. The flower buds of a bush, *Capparis spinosa*. These buds are packed in salt or pickled and used in sauces, on pizzas and as a general flavouring. The salted variety should be soaked for 10–15 minutes and drained well. Pickled capers simply need to be well drained.

Ceci. Chickpeas, also known as garbanzo beans.

Crostini. Small rounds of bread toasted and spread with a variety of toppings or just used for dipping. They are served as part of the antipasto.

Dried mushrooms. This usually refers to dried porcini, which is a type of mushroom. These are among the richest flavoured of all mushrooms and so only a small amount is required in most recipes.

Fettuccine. Ribbons of pasta. Both dried and fresh fettuccine are available in several different colours and flavours at your grocery store. On most pasta machines a cutter for fettuccine-sized pasta is a standard feature.

Fettunta. The Tuscan name for a thick slice of bread toasted and brushed with extra virgin olive oil and often rubbed with garlic after toasting. In Umbria the same thing is called bruschetta.

Focaccia. A flat yeast bread made in Liguria and now popular here. In Tuscany it is called schiacciata.

Frittata. Italian for omelette. Cooked in a heavy-bottomed pan, it is served flat, often in wedges.

Fusilli. Spirals of dried pasta. Available from the grocery store in the dried pasta section, they come in all sorts of different colours and flavours.

Garlic. A strong-smelling bulb (*Allium sativum*) of the lily family. It adds flavour and character to foods and there is strong evidence that it is good for you as well.

Grappa. A strong Italian brandy.

Grissini. Long, crisp bread sticks from the Piedmont area.

Gnocchi. Pronounced 'noki', these are dumplings made of potato, bread, flours or vegetables.

Gorgonzola. A green vein mould cheese made with full cream milk. Both mild and strong varieties are available.

Herbs. The unique flavours we have come to associate with a particular country's cuisine are partly the result of certain traditional combinations of herbs. In Italy these herbs include basil, Italian parsley, sage, tarragon, marjoram and oregano. Herbs are used fresh wherever possible.

Italian parsley. With its flat leaves, this parsley is easier to deal with than traditional parsley. It also has a stronger flavour. Use it in Italian cooking if you have it in your garden (where it will grow happily).

Lemoncello. A clean and neat citrus aperitif served chilled. It is delicious over ice cream, used in desserts or just as it comes.

Marjoram and oregano. *Majorama hortensis* and *Origanum vulgare* are quite similar in taste but are certainly different herbs. Marjoram has a lighter, more subtle flavour, whereas oregano is stronger and more bold. Use fresh if possible or buy small quantities dried as they don't keep their flavour well in storage.

Macceroni. Dried pasta tubes. They may be ribbed or smooth, bent or straight. Available in all grocery stores in the dried pasta section.

Marsala. A particularly delicious sherry-like wine originally from Sicily. Often used in desserts and sauces.

Mascarpone. A rich creamy cheese with a smooth, sweet, slightly acid taste. Most like clotted cream in consistency, it is used mainly in dessert dishes. In New Zealand mascarpone is made by Mahoe Farmhouse Cheeses, Kapiti Cheeses and Miranda Valley Cheeses. You may need to ask for this cheese to be ordered for you at the deli counter of your supermarket.

Mortadella. A large pork sausage made in Bologna. Often used on antipasto platters or in a sandwich and has a smooth texture and delicate flavour.

Mozzarella. A soft white cheese used for its melting quality, mozzarella was originally made from buffaloes' milk but nowadays it is made from cows' milk and is called fior di latte. Mozzarella fior di latte should be moist and eaten quite fresh. If it dries out a bit, it is called mozzarella scamorze. Mozzarella is used on pizzas, in sauces and other cooked dishes. Mozzarella bocconcini ('little mouthfuls') are shaped into smaller balls and are stored in a light brine or in their own whey; they too, are eaten fresh, within 2 weeks of being made. Several New Zealand companies make mozzarella fior di latte, which is readily available in the dairy section of your supermarket.

Mushrooms. See dried mushrooms.

Oil. Aside from olive oil, sunflower seed oil is the oil most commonly used for Italian cooking, particularly where the distinctive taste of olive oil is not required.

Olives. Olives come in a variety of types, from small olives with large pits, such as the French Niçoise, to large, fleshy olives such as the Chilean Azapa brand. Generally, the ripe black olives are pressed for their oil while both the unripe green and the black olives are used whole or chopped in cooking. Both green and black olives may be preserved in brine or in oil; they may be pitted or unpitted and are sometimes stuffed with almonds, pimentos or anchovies. They may also be marinated in herbs and spices such as coriander, lemon juice, chilli, thyme, ginger and garlic.

To preserve your own olives in brine, soak the freshly picked fruit in water for 10 days, changing the water daily, then bottle in plain brine (about 50% saturated) with a sprig of rosemary. They will take some months to lose their bitter taste. Then they can be stored in flavoured oil.

Generally the large black olives, such as Pelion or Kalamata brands, are soft and taste rather sharp. The Spanish brands, on the other hand, are firmer and have a more mild, even bland taste. It all comes down to personal taste but I think that the sharper tasting olives are more exciting and are the best type for eating whole, in salads, on pizzas or on antipasto platters. The more bland olives should be combined with other ingredients, e.g. in a tapenade. When buying olives from the deli don't hesitate to ask to try one to be sure they are the type you are after.

Olive oils. The main factor which distinguishes the various oils is their acid content. The finer and more expensive oils are the extra virgin and virgin olive oils. Extra virgin olive oil is obtained from a cold pressing of the olives. This is usually their first pressing, hence the interesting name. This is the best oil to use for raw foods such as salads or in dips. Robust and fruity, this oil has no acid aftertaste. It is very low in acid (less than 1%) and there is some indication that it actually helps to dissolve cholesterol in the blood.

The subsequent pressing of the remaining pits and flesh yields the lesser oils, which can have an unpleasant acid aftertaste. Tuscany is said to produce the best olive oils.

On the whole, try to use extra virgin olive oil as the flavour adds an important quality to Italian food. There is no substitute for genuine Italian extra virgin olive oil.

Pancetta. Italian bacon which has been cured but not smoked.

It is rolled into sausage shapes and sold in thin slices.

Panettone. Italy's famous Christmas bread from Milan, this is a sweet bread similar to the French brioche and is served at breakfast with coffee or after dinner with wine.

Panforte. A rich, heavy cake made with fruit, nuts, chocolate and honey, this keeps well and improves with age.

Parmesan. See parmigiano.

Parmigiano. The correct Italian name for what we call parmesan cheese. A hard and granular cheese made from cows' milk. The best Italian parmesan is produced in the Parma-Reggio area. Italian-made parmesan is expensive but worth it. The cheese has been matured for at least 2 years and the flavour is so concentrated that a tablespoon or so is all that is required to flavour a dish.

Never buy your parmesan grated. A wedge of it keeps better and should be grated shortly before use. New Zealand parmesans, adequate for soups, sauces and pastas, are constantly improving, so we should soon have a local product that is just as good — and perhaps cheaper.

Pasta. Literally boiled dough, pasta, surprisingly, became the universal Italian dish only about 70 years ago. For soups choose tiny shapes such as alphabets, bows or shells. For boiling, choose flat noodles, round solid types or tubular types such as maccheroni and rigatoni. For stuffing and baking use ravioli, tortellini, lasagna or cannelloni.

Available in either electric or manual types, pasta machines roll and cut the pasta dough in a fraction of the time it takes to roll it out with a rolling pin and cut it with a knife.

Pecorino. A ewes'-milk cheese (pecora is the Italian word for sheep) with a slightly salty flavour. There are different names for pecorino, which is made in different areas and from different breeds of sheep. Pecorino massese comes from Massa and has a very delicate curd. Pecorino romano, which is said to be the best, has a harder grain and a sharper flavour. Pecorino goes particularly well with fresh pears as a refreshing and light dessert.

In many recipes you may substitute parmesan for pecorino. Romano-style pecorino is available in the dairy sections of supermarkets.

Penne. Dried tubes of pasta cut at an angle like nibs of a pen. They can be small or large, ribbed or smooth, and are used in the same type of dishes as you would use maccheroni. Available in all good grocery stores.

Pomodori secchi. Sun-dried tomatoes preserved in oil with herbs. (Both olive and other types of oil are used.) The flavour of the sweet, ripe tomatoes is concentrated and they are real flavour bursts when cut in strips in a salad or put on an antipasto plate. Sometimes sun-dried tomatoes are packed without oil, but these, in my view, are vastly inferior. They are not as versatile and should be used in sauces or in dishes where they can be reconstituted slightly before eating.

Prosciutto. Ham cured by drying, not smoking, it may be raw (crudo) or cooked (cotto). Prosciutto crudo is an unsmoked salt-cured ham cut into very thin slices, often served with melon. It should be sliced thinly lengthwise, parallel to the bone.

Polenta. Made from cornmeal and water and cooked to a thick porridge which is then allowed to set, polenta is cut into squares or circles and served with a sauce, or worked to make savoury fried cakes or baked rounds.

Provolone. This cheese is a tastier version of mozzarella, for which it can be substituted.

Ravioli. Little pillows of pasta that are filled with meat or vegetable fillings. They are easy and rewarding to make but can also be bought fresh in the refrigerated section of the grocery store.

Ricotta. A soft unsalted cheese made with cows' milk (though originally it was a ewes' milk cheese). Store in the refrigerator and use for desserts, with pasta and eaten fresh like cottage cheese.

Rigatoni. Ribbed tubes of pasta, generally larger than maccheroni but smaller than cannelloni, and filled with meat or vegetable filling.

Risotto. Rice cooked in stock. Arborio rice is most often used to make this dish since it will absorb a lot of the stock and still remain al dente (firm to the bite).

Saffron. Saffron, the stamens of a crocus (*Crocus sativus*), is used to give dishes a yellow colour and a particularly rich and earthy flavour. Turmeric is sometimes used as a cheaper substitute; it will give you a yellow colour but it has none of saffron's flavour. Although proper saffron is expensive, ground saffron, which is one grade down from that, is perfectly acceptable and without doubt a better choice than turmeric.

Sambucca. A liquorice-flavoured liqueur excellent in zabaglione, chocolate desserts, cream pies, puddings and mousses. As an aperitif it is sometimes served aflame with a coffee bean floating on it.

Schiacciata. Pronounced 'scotchy-ata', a flat yeast bread from Tuscany, also called focaccia elsewhere in Italy. It is seasoned with salt and oil, plus sometimes rosemary or sage.

Tagliatelle. The name given to a wide-ribbon pasta made in north and central Italy. It is similar to fettuccine but wider.

Tomatoes. Italians grow either the San Marzano plum tomato or the Marmande tomato, both of which are very flavourful and rich in colour. An indispensable ingredient in Italian cuisine, these tomatoes are available peeled in tins, which are very convenient. Locally grown tomatoes, both outdoor and hothouse varieties, are usually good. During winter I recommend using tinned tomatoes rather than the flavourless imported Australian tomatoes.

Tomato paste and tomato purée should be part of your standard pantry items since they can be readily substituted for tomatoes in many recipes.

Tortellini. Small squares of pasta filled and folded in half and then pinched together around the finger to form a little hat shape. This is the Tuscan name for cappelletti.

Antipasti
Appetisers

Antipasti are what we call appetisers: an antipasto is the little bite before the meal – pasto is the Italian word for meal and anti means 'that which comes before'. You can serve any of these dishes as individual portions like entrées or fill a platter with an array of tasty titbits for the more classic antipasto arrangement. Whatever you choose for this pre-meal, they should be small quantities of very tasty food, designed to get your taste buds into a state of anticipation about the meal to come.

Just as we wouldn't normally set out chips and dip before an everyday family dinner, so an antipasto platter isn't presented before an ordinary Italian evening meal. When you do have occasion to put together some antipasti, however, make sure that they complement and do not detract from the flavours of the upcoming meal.

Bocconcini fritti
Deep-fried bocconcini

Bocconcini are small balls of mozzarella. The parmesan is necessary to give this dish more flavour while the bocconcini adds a delightful 'stretchy' quality. Serve warm but not hot, on their own or with the chilli mayonnaise to dip them in.

250 g bocconcini (about 20)
1 cup dried breadcrumbs
$1/4$ cup parsley, chopped
$1/2$ cup parmesan, grated
flour
1 egg
2 tablespoons milk
olive oil

Chilli mayonnaise
1 egg
1 teaspoon chilli powder
2 tablespoons balsamic vinegar
1 cup extra virgin olive oil

Dry the bocconcini lightly and toss in the flour. Mix the breadcrumbs, parsley and parmesan together. Dip the floured bocconcini in the beaten egg and milk and roll in the breadcrumb mixture.

Place them in the freezer while you heat enough oil to cover the bocconcini. Deep-fry them for about 1 minute or until golden. Drain on absorbent paper and serve warm.

Make the chilli mayonnaise by putting the egg, chilli powder, vinegar and half of the oil in a blender. Turn it on and slowly add the remaining oil. Blend until the mayonnaise is thick, about 25 seconds from beginning to end.

Carciofi con salsa d'acciughe
Artichokes with anchovy sauce

2–4 washed and trimmed fresh artichokes
6 anchovy fillets
2 teaspoons spring onion, finely chopped
2 teaspoons prepared mustard
$^1/_4$ cup extra virgin olive oil
$^1/_4$ cup cider vinegar

Cook the artichokes in boiling water until a leaf can easily be pulled from the head (typically about 15 minutes). Drain and keep warm.

Put the remaining ingredients into a blender and purée to a smooth paste.

Pour the sauce into a bowl and place the artichokes around it so that people can pull off leaves and dip them in the sauce.

Bagna cauda
Hot cream and anchovy dip

This is an absolutely delicious dip that is served warm, for example in a dish over a simmering fondue pot of water. Raw vegetables (and perhaps pieces of bread or crostini) are dipped into it. Or it may be served as a sauce for pasta. The name means 'hot bath'.

50 g butter
4 cloves garlic, crushed
45 g (a small tin) anchovy fillets, drained and chopped
600 ml cream
vegetables for dipping: carrot strips, celery sticks, cauliflower florets and button mushrooms

Melt the butter in a pot and add the garlic and the well-drained and chopped anchovy fillets. Fry briefly and then pour in the cream. Bring to the boil, reduce the heat and simmer gently, stirring occasionally, until the sauce thickens. This should take about 30 minutes.

Crostini
Little toasts

These little toasted rounds of bread are so simple to make, and delicious served topped with all sorts of tasty goodies such as pestos, anchovies and cheese, fresh tomatoes and basil . . . use your imagination!

1 loaf french bread
extra virgin olive oil

Slice the bread into rounds about 2 cm thick and place on a baking tray. Brush with the olive oil and toast under the griller until golden. Remove from the oven, turn the slices over and brush with oil. Toast under the griller until golden. Cool completely and store in an airtight container until required.

Bruschetta o fettunta al pomodoro e basilico
Tomatoes and basil on toast

This is quite simply slices of fettunta or bruschetta (types of Italian bread), toasted and topped with chopped fresh tomatoes and basil. It is the juxtaposition of the warm toast and cold tomatoes, as much as the combination of flavours, that makes this dish so special.

firm ripe tomatoes
fresh basil
crusty bread (e.g. french bread stick)

Place slices of bread on a baking sheet and grill in the oven, turning once to toast both sides. Rub a cut clove of garlic over one side of the toast and brush lightly with oil. Arrange the toasts on a platter and place a slice of tomato and leaf of fresh basil on each. Serve immediately.

Note: In the Apulia region this is made with ruchetta, a type of rocket or salad herb belonging to the mustard family, instead of basil.

Melanzane alla griglia
Grilled eggplant

This is served as a cold appetiser eaten as is.

1 eggplant
parsley
garlic
extra virgin olive oil

Slice the eggplant, place it on a baking tray and grill lightly until tender and a light golden colour. In a serving dish layer the grilled eggplant, parsley, crushed garlic and generous amounts of the olive oil. Let stand for at least 2 hours, turning once during that time.

Peperonata
Pepper stew

This is a hot antipasto often served with a piece of focaccia or on top of crostini.

3 peppers of different colours, chopped coarsely
$^1/_4$ cup olive oil
3 cloves garlic, crushed
1 onion, chopped coarsely
2 tomatoes, peeled and chopped
1 tablespoon fresh oregano, finely chopped

Sauté the onion and garlic in the oil until transparent. Add the peppers and tomatoes and simmer gently until peppers are tender. Sprinkle with oregano and serve.

Peperoni alle acciughe
Peppers with anchovies

This is a cold antipasto.

3 peppers of different colours
4 anchovy fillets, chopped
1 tablespoon fresh oregano, chopped
2 cloves garlic, thinly sliced
1 tablespoon capers, drained
$^1/_4$ cup extra virgin olive oil

Pre-heat the oven to 200° C. Wash, quarter and de-seed the peppers and bake 15–20 minutes. Remove from the oven and allow to cool. Cut into strips.

Place the peppers on a serving dish and sprinkle with the remaining ingredients, plus salt if desired. Let stand for about 2 hours before serving.

Olive fritte
Fried olives

This is a delicious taste sensation where the crunchy breadcrumb crust contrasts with the salty, firm texture of the olives and prepares the palate for a smoother cheesy or creamy next course. Fried olives are served warm, either 2 or 3 on individual plates or on an antipasto platter. They are particularly good with a dry white wine.

10–12 large green olives
$^1/_2$ cup flour
1 egg, lightly beaten
$^1/_2$ cup dried breadcrumbs
2 tablespoons parmesan, finely grated
olive oil for frying

Drain the olives. Put the flour and olives into a small bag and shake together. Remove the olives, shake off any extra flour and dip them in the beaten egg.

Mix the breadcrumbs and parmesan and then roll the olives in this mixture.

Heat the oil (it should be deep enough to cover the olives while frying) and fry a few olives at a time until they are golden (about 30 seconds). Remove and drain well on absorbent paper. Serve warm.

Funghi ripieni alla griglia
Grilled filled mushrooms

250–300 g large button mushrooms
4 rashers bacon
2 cloves garlic
$^1/_4$ cup parmesan, grated
1 tablespoon parsley, chopped
1 tablespoon capers, well drained
3 tablespoons dried breadcrumbs
pinch dried oregano
olive oil

Clean the mushrooms and remove the stalks. Chop the bacon finely. Put the remaining ingredients into a food processor and whizz to combine. Add enough olive oil to make a smooth mixture. Add the bacon and whizz briefly to combine.

Fill the mushroom caps and place on a baking tray and drizzle with a little oil. Grill for 4-6 minutes or until golden. Serve warm.

Peperoni arrosto
Grilled peppers

Serve with crostini or fresh schiacciata. They are also nice as a side dish to the main meal.

$^1/_4$ cup extra virgin olive oil
5 cloves garlic, chopped
1 tablespoon fresh basil, finely chopped
5 large capsicums of assorted colours
salt and pepper

Mix the oil, garlic and basil together in a jar and allow to stand while you prepare the capsicums.

Cut the capsicums into quarters and remove the seeds and white membrane. Place on a rack and grill, turning once to brown both sides. Remove from the oven and place in a shallow serving dish.

Sprinkle with salt and freshly ground pepper. Shake the oil mixture and drizzle over the capsicums. Serve warm or cold.

Crostini alle olive con funghi
Toasted bread with olives and mushrooms

This dish is small rounds of toasted french bread (the crostini) spread with puréed olives and sautéed mushrooms, all served warm from the grill for a beautiful cocktail treat or a stunning appetiser.

$^1/_2$ cup black olives, pitted
1 long french loaf
$1^1/_2$ cups extra virgin olive oil
300 g mushrooms, chopped
2 cloves garlic, crushed
$^1/_4$ cup olive oil
salt and pepper

Purée the olives in a food processor and set aside. To make the crostini, slice the french bread into rounds about 2 cm thick and dip them in the extra virgin olive oil. Then place them on a rack in a baking pan and toast under the grill until golden. Turn and toast the other side, taking care not to burn them.

Some oil will drain out of the bread while it is toasting. You can collect this and use it for frying later. When both sides are toasted, remove them from the tray and place on a paper towel to soak up any extra oil.

Fry the mushrooms and garlic in the oil and season to taste.

To assemble, spread each crostini with about a teaspoon of olive purée, then spread another teaspoon of the fried mushrooms on top. Place on a baking tray, grill lightly to warm through, and serve immediately.

Pomodori ripieni
Stuffed tomatoes

1 punnet ripe cherry tomatoes
1 cup fresh basil leaves
1 clove garlic, crushed
$^1/_4$ cup pine nuts
2 tablespoons parmesan, grated
$^1/_4$ cup olive oil

Cut the tops off the tomatoes and gently squeeze out the seeds. Turn upside down to drain for about 30 minutes.

Purée the remaining ingredients to make the pesto. Fill the tomatoes with the pesto, arrange on a plate and garnish with extra basil leaves. This makes about 35.

Olive oil for dipping

The rich and full flavour of extra virgin olive oil makes a wonderful base for dipping schiacciata or any other fresh bread. It's worthwhile trying several different brands of oil to find the one you like best. By adding your choice of dried herbs and spices you can create your own special blend.

Remember that if you're keeping the flavoured oil for more than a day or so you must use dried herbs since any fresh herbs that stick out of the oil will quickly grow mould. To serve, pour the oil into a small bowl and place it in the centre of a platter with slices of fresh bread around it for dipping. Here are some suggested combinations.

A little spicy
1 cup extra virgin olive oil
1 dried red chilli
1 sprig dried rosemary
1 sprig dried oregano

Place all ingredients in a jar and leave at least 24 hours to flavour through before serving.

Garlic and sage oil
1 cup extra virgin olive oil
2 sprigs dried sage
3 cloves garlic

Place all ingredients in a jar and leave at least 24 hours to flavour through before serving.

Peppery oil
1 cup extra virgin olive oil
5 whole peppercorns
1 dried bay leaf

Place all ingredients in a jar and leave at least 24 hours to flavour through before serving.

Single-herb oils
Combine a cup of extra virgin olive oil with any one of these fresh herbs — basil, oregano, mint, Italian parsley or dill — and let stand for a few hours, then strain out the herb and serve.

Tapenade alle olive
Olive and anchovy dip

Serve this cold dip made of puréed olives, anchovies and garlic with crackers, crostini or bread sticks. It keeps well and, because the flavours develop, can (and should) be made a day in advance. Any left over is great on toast for lunch the next day.

250 g black olives, pitted
50 g anchovies, drained
1 clove garlic
2 tablespoons olive oil
2 tablespoons lemon juice

Blend all the ingredients in a food processor until you have a fine but not totally puréed texture. Store in glass jars in the refrigerator until required.

Tapenade ai fichi
Fig and anchovy purée

This is best made with fresh figs. Alternatively, use dried figs that you have soaked in water for 30 minutes.

1 x 45 g tin anchovies, well drained
40–50 fresh figs or 50 g dried figs, soaked in water to cover for 30 minutes
6 cloves garlic

Whizz all the ingredients in a food processor to produce a coarse and even-textured mixture. Store in a jar in the refrigerator until required.

Contorni e zuppe
Side dishes and soups

Side dishes

A frittata is an omelette made in the Italian way. It is often served as a light meal preceded by a light soup, but can also be a course in a more substantial meal. A frittata is cooked slowly over a low heat so that the whole thing is firm and completely cooked — unlike an omelette, which is meant to be slightly undercooked and a little runny — and a frittata is served flat, perhaps cut into wedges, whereas an omelette is folded.

Make frittata using any combination of ingredients you would for an omelette, following the method outlined in the recipes for lettuce or cheese frittata (see page 30).

Gnocchi are little dumplings made with potatoes, bread, spinach or semolina. Rather bland on their own, they are always served with a sauce or a tasty grated cheese such as parmesan or gorgonzola. They may also be dotted with butter and grated cheese and baked.

There are many ways of shaping gnocchi but I find it easiest simply to roll the dough into a sausage shape slightly thicker than your thumb and cut it into short (2 cm) lengths.

Canederli
Bread gnocchi

Little bread dumplings, these may be served as a soup in a broth or as an accompaniment to a main dish. Any leftover bread gnocchi are very nice fried in butter.

500 g stale bread, cubed
2 cups milk
25 g butter
1 onion, finely chopped
1 tablespoon thyme, chopped
pinch ground nutmeg
3 eggs
8 cups broth (see pages 32–34)
100 g butter
$\frac{1}{2}$ cup parmesan, grated

Soak the bread in the milk for 10 minutes, drain and squeeze out moisture. Melt the butter and sauté the onion. Add the onions, thyme, nutmeg and eggs to the bread and mix well.

Bring the broth to the boil and drop tablespoonfuls of the mixture into it. Bring the stock back to the boil, reduce heat, cover and simmer 10 minutes. Remove with a slotted spoon onto a serving plate and keep warm.

Heat the butter until it colours, pour over the gnocchi and sprinkle with cheese.

Note: If your gnocchi fall apart while cooking, add some flour to the dough to make it firmer.

Gnocchi di spinaci
Spinach gnocchi

There is really no substitute for ricotta cheese to create the right flavour and texture in this recipe and, happily, ricotta is now widely available.

500 g fresh spinach
20 g butter
$^1/_2$ small onion, chopped
2 rashers bacon, chopped
250 g ricotta cheese
$^1/_2$ cup parmesan, grated
1 egg
$^3/_4$ cup flour
pinch ground nutmeg

Wash the spinach and remove any hard stalks. Bring a pot of salted water to the boil and add the spinach. Bring the water back to the boil and then drain the spinach well. Squeeze out as much water as you can and chop finely.

Melt the butter in a large frying pan and sauté the onion and bacon until the bacon begins to brown and the onion is tender. Remove from the heat and add the chopped spinach.

Put this mixture into a bowl and add the ricotta, parmesan, egg, flour and nutmeg. Mix well and shape into ovals about the size of large walnuts. You may need to add extra flour so that you can work the dough.

Bring a pot of salted water to the boil and drop in a few gnocchi at a time. When the water returns to the boil time it for 2 minutes, then remove the gnocchi with a slotted spoon and place in a baking dish while you cook the rest.

Pour the melted butter over the gnocchi and sprinkle with the grated parmesan. Bake at 190°C for 5 minutes or until the cheese has melted. Remove from the oven and allow to cool for a few minutes before serving. Serve with a bowl of extra grated parmesan alongside.

Gnocchi di patate
Potato gnocchi

These little potato dumplings are made mostly in the Piedmont area of Italy. For best results use a red potato such as Desiree or Red Rascal.

3 cups warm mashed potatoes
$1^1/_2$ cups flour
1 tablespoon olive oil
2 eggs

Mash the potatoes together with the flour, oil and eggs. Tip onto a counter and knead to a smooth consistency. Roll into thin sausage shapes and cut into 2 cm pieces. Cook the gnocchi by dropping about a third of them into boiling salted water and cooking a further 5 minutes after they rise to the surface. Drain and place in a baking dish.

Cover with sauce (see pages 48-54 for sauce suggestions) and bake for 10-15 minutes at 180°C. Or try dotting them with butter and grated cheese before baking.

Tortino di polenta e parmigiano
Polenta with cheese

This is the traditional way of serving polenta. Remember that polenta on its own is quite bland and needs a sauce or good cheese to dress it up. You can also use provolone or any tasty cheese you prefer.

3$\frac{1}{2}$ cups (400 g) ground cornmeal (maize flour)
150 g parmesan cheese
2 tablespoons butter
2 litres water

Stir the cornmeal into the water. Bring to the boil then reduce heat and simmer 45 minutes, stirring occasionally. Add the butter and allow to cool in a dish, then cut into slices.

Layer the polenta and cheese and drizzle with extra oil and bake at 230°C until crisp.

Polenta con limatura
Filled polenta

If you are using bought vegetable stock concentrate then I recommend Vecon, which is very flavourful and low in salt. It is still best, however, to make your own broth whenever possible.

2 cups finely ground cornmeal
8 cups vegetable broth (see page 32) or
   8 cups hot water and 4 teaspoons vegetable stock
   powder
1 tablespoon extra virgin olive oil
$\frac{1}{2}$ cup parmesan, grated
3 tablespoons fresh basil or parsley, chopped
12–15 fresh basil leaves
6–8 slices prosciutto
$\frac{1}{2}$ cup sun-dried tomatoes, coarsely chopped
12 slices mozzarella
1 cup parmesan, grated

Bring the stock to the boil and stir in the cornmeal and oil. Simmer gently for 15-20 minutes, stirring occasionally so that it doesn't stick to the bottom of the pot. Remove from the heat and stir in the $\frac{1}{2}$ cup of parmesan cheese and chopped basil. Oil a lamington pan (approximately 20 x 30 cm) and spread the polenta mixture evenly in it. Allow to set in the refrigerator for about an hour.

Turn polenta out onto a baking tray lined with baking paper and slice it in half so that you have two pieces, each 20 x 30 cm. Layer with the basil leaves, then the prosciutto, then the sun-dried tomatoes and finally the thin slices of mozzarella. Place the second layer of polenta on top and sprinkle with the cup of parmesan. Bake at 230°C for 30 minutes. If the mozzarella isn't golden when cooked you can briefly grill to crisp it up.

Torta di verdure
Sweet spinach pie

This is lovely as a light meal or even as a dessert. It looks beautiful and, since it is served warm or even cold, it is very practical for buffets.

Pastry
2 cups flour
2 tablespoons sugar
125 g butter
2 eggs
water

Filling
2 tablespoons extra virgin olive oil
1¹/₂ cups zucchini, chopped
3-4 cups raw spinach, chopped
¹/₄ cup pine nuts
2 tablespoons raisins
1 tablespoon sugar
1 egg
1 tablespoon candied peel

3 tablespoons parmesan, grated
¹/₂ teaspoon cinnamon

To make the pastry, put all the ingredients into a food processor and whizz. Tip out onto the benchtop and knead together, adding water as needed to make a smooth and firm dough that is not sticky. Cover and leave in the refrigerator while you make the filling.

Heat the oil in a large frying pan and sauté the zucchini and spinach until tender. Remove from the heat, stir in the remaining ingredients and allow to cool.

Pre-heat the oven to 190°C. Line a 23 cm pie dish with half of the pastry and add the cooled filling. Roll out the remaining pastry, cut into strips and lattice them over the top of the pie. Brush with a beaten egg and bake for 25–30 minutes. Remove from the oven and allow to cool before serving.

Tuoni lampo
Thunder and lightning

250 g chickpeas, soaked overnight in cold water
250 g small pasta shapes
¹/₄ cup butter or extra virgin olive oil or
   1 cup tomato sauce (see recipe on page 53)

Cook the chickpeas until soft (about 1-2 hours), then drain. Cook the pasta according to the instructions on the packet, drain and mix with the cooked chickpeas. Toss together with the butter or sauce and serve sprinkled with parmesan.

Frittata al formaggio
Cheese omelette

A frittata differs from an omelette in that it is cooked slowly until completely firm and then served cut into wedges or as a whole flat piece. If you don't have a non-stick pan then a heavy-bottomed one is fine since it distributes the heat well.

50 g butter
8 eggs
salt and pepper
1 cup parmesan, grated

Melt the butter in a 25-30 cm non-stick frying pan. Beat the eggs, salt and pepper and parmesan together and, when the butter is hot, pour in the egg mixture and turn the heat down low.

Cook slowly until it is just browned on the bottom and almost set through. Pre-heat the grill to high and place the pan under it for 20-30 seconds to finish the cooking.

Frittata di lattuga
Lettuce omelette

This is the Italian version of a French omelette — or perhaps it was the other way around!

3 tablespoons extra virgin olive oil
2 spring onions, sliced
3 packed cups sliced lettuce
$1/4$ cup Marsala or dry sherry
salt and pepper
8 eggs, beaten
$1/4$ cup parmesan, grated

Heat the oil in a non-stick frying pan and sauté the onion and lettuce, stirring constantly so they don't burn. Pour in the Marsala and season with salt and pepper and simmer for 2 minutes. Meanwhile beat the eggs and parmesan together and then pour this mixture over the lettuce and stir together briefly.

Cover and cook on low heat until the bottom of the omelette is golden. Uncover and place the pan under the griller and cook for 20-30 seconds until the top of the omelette is golden. Slide onto a serving plate and sprinkle with a little extra grated parmesan.

Ceci allo zafferano
Chickpeas with saffron

*This creamy chickpea stew can be served as a simple
vegetarian meal by itself or as a dish to accompany other
food. The amount of chilli can and should be varied to
suit your taste.*

500 g chickpeas, soaked overnight in cold water
3 tablespoons olive oil
1 onion, chopped
3 tomatoes, peeled and chopped
1 teaspoon chilli powder or
   1 small hot red chilli, chopped
salt and pepper
$^{1}/_{4}$ teaspoon saffron or turmeric

Drain the chickpeas, put into a pot, cover with salted water
and bring to the boil. Reduce heat and simmer for $1^{1}/_{2}$ hours
or until cooked. Drain and reserve $^{1}/_{2}$ cup of the liquid.

Heat the oil in a pan and sauté the onion, then add the
chickpeas, tomatoes, chilli powder, saffron or turmeric and
reserved liquid from the chickpeas. Reduce the heat and
simmer gently for 30 minutes.

You may need to add a little extra hot water during this
second cooking time, but be careful not to add much. There
should be only a very little saucy liquid with the chickpeas
when you have finished cooking.

Pezzelle di pane
Cheese on toast

*Leave it to the Italians to make cheese on toast into an
art form. This is a good example of how to take an old
favourite and treat it in an Italian way. Substitute your
favourite cheese for the mozzarella if you prefer.*

4–6 thick slices day-old bread
1 cup milk
$^{1}/_{4}$ cup olive oil
2 cloves garlic, crushed
6 fresh or canned tomatoes, peeled
1 teaspoon oregano (fresh is best)
salt and pepper
250 g mozzarella

Lay the slices of bread in a shallow baking dish and pour over
the milk. Heat the oil in a frying pan and cook the garlic,
tomatoes and oregano until the tomatoes are soft. Season
with salt and pepper.

Spoon this mixture over the bread and arrange slices of
mozzarella on top. Bake at 180°C for 15–20 minutes until
mozzarella is melted and golden.

Soups

Perhaps the best-known Italian soup is minestrone, a thick vegetable soup which often has pasta or rice added. Italian soups have a number of different regional names. Minestra is the Italian word for soup, but whereas a broth in Tuscany would be called cacciucco, on the opposite coast the same sort of thing would be called brodo.

Brodo is similar to the French stock but is less concentrated. It's a good idea to make up a quantity of broth and freeze it so that you can simply pull out what you need when a recipe calls for it. Stock cubes or powder are a convenient shortcut but recipes certainly taste better if made with your own broth.

A bowl of grated parmesan is often put on the table with soups as an additional garnish. For some soups, such as potato and onion soup, a small bottle or bowl of chilli oil might be provided to give that strong flavour contrast.

Brodo di verdure
Vegetable broth

Use this as a stock or as a clear broth soup.

1 tablespoon extra virgin olive oil
1 onion, chopped
3 carrots, chopped
1 stalk celery, chopped
400 g fresh or canned tomatoes, peeled
2 large potatoes, peeled and cubed
1 tablespoon fresh basil, chopped
1 teaspoon sea salt
pinch freshly ground pepper
1½ litres water

Heat the oil in a large saucepan and sauté the onion, carrots and celery until they are soft. Add the tomatoes, potatoes, basil, salt and pepper and continue cooking for a few minutes. Add the water and bring to the boil. Reduce the heat and simmer gently for 20-30 minutes or until the potatoes are soft. Strain out the vegetables and store the broth until required.

You may also make this as a vegetable soup by puréeing the vegetables and returning them to the broth. Serve with grated parmesan.

Brodo di pesce
Fish broth

Use this as a stock or as a clear broth soup. Preferably use fish-heads and trimmings rather than fillets — they give a tastier broth and are cheaper. Ideal fish for stock include snapper, groper, blue cod, warehou and bluenose.

2 litres water
1 kg fish pieces
2 cloves garlic
4 tablespoons olive oil
2 anchovy fillets, chopped
1 tablespoon parsley, chopped
400 g fresh or canned tomatoes, peeled
1 onion, chopped
1 carrot, chopped
1 celery stalk, chopped
2 teaspoons sea salt

Add all the ingredients to a large saucepan and bring to the boil. Reduce the heat and simmer gently for 15–20 minutes. Remove from the heat and strain into a clean jar. Ensure you use a strainer that is fine enough to catch all the scales and small bones. Store broth in the refrigerator until required.

Brodo di carne
Beef broth

Use this as a stock or as a clear broth soup.

2 litres water
1 kg beef marrow bones
500 g chuck steak
2 carrots, chopped
1 onion, chopped
1 stalk celery, chopped
2 teaspoons sea salt
$\frac{1}{2}$ teaspoon freshly ground pepper
1 bay leaf
400 g fresh or canned tomatoes, peeled

Put all ingredients in a large saucepan and bring to the boil. Reduce the heat and simmer gently for 3–4 hours with the lid on. Remove from the heat, strain into a clean jar and store in the refrigerator until required.

Brodo di pollo
Chicken broth

Use this as a stock or as a clear broth soup.

2 kg chicken frames and pieces
1 carrot, chopped
1 stalk celery, chopped
400 g fresh or canned tomatoes, peeled
2 teaspoons sea salt
$1/4$ teaspoon freshly ground pepper
1 small bay leaf
$2^1/_2$ litres water

Put all the ingredients into a large saucepan and bring to the boil. Reduce the heat and simmer gently for 1 hour. Strain and reserve the liquid in a clean jar in the refrigerator until required.

Minestra di broccoli e pasta
Broccoli and pasta soup

3 rashers fatty bacon
3 cloves garlic, mashed
$1/2$ teaspoon ground dried chilli
2 cups broccoli florets
$1/2$ litre white wine
1 litre water
3 cups uncooked small pasta
grated parmesan

Chop the bacon coarsely and cook for a few minutes in a large pot. Add the garlic, chilli, broccoli and wine and toss, then bring to the boil. Add the water and bring back to the boil. Now add the pasta and boil until it is cooked, about 10 minutes. Adjust the seasoning and serve with a generous grating of parmesan on top.

Minestrone di manzo
Hearty beef soup

A thick soup made with lots of different vegetables and pasta or rice. Different sorts of meats may also be used, such as ham, beef, smoked pork spare ribs or frankfurters. It is also important to garnish with lots of parmesan for that authentic Italian touch.

2 tablespoons extra virgin olive oil
250 g gravy beef, cubed
3 cloves garlic, chopped
1 large onion, finely sliced
2 large carrots, peeled and finely chopped
1 cup french beans, coarsely chopped
3 tomatoes, peeled and chopped
2 litres beef broth (see page 33) or
   2 litres hot water and 3 teaspoons beef stock
   powder
2 tablespoons tomato paste
1 cup dried haricot beans
1 cup uncooked small pasta
1 tablespoon basil pesto (see page 51) or
   2 teaspoons basil (fresh is best)
$1/2$ cup parmesan, grated

Heat the oil in a large pot and brown the meat on all sides. Add the garlic, onion, carrots, beans, tomatoes, beef broth (or water and beef stock powder), tomato paste and beans and bring to the boil. Reduce the heat and simmer gently for 1–2 hours or until the beans are cooked. If more liquid is required add some water or more broth at this stage.

Add the pasta and cook a further 15–20 minutes or until the pasta is cooked. Add the pesto or basil and adjust the seasoning if required with salt and pepper. Serve warm garnished with plenty of grated parmesan and hunks of fresh bread.

Zuppa di pesce
Fish soup

Every little town on the Italian coast has its own fish soup recipe. The more varieties of fish you use, the more interesting the soup tastes.

1/4 cup extra virgin olive oil
1 small onion, chopped
1 carrot, peeled and chopped
1 stalk celery, chopped
1/2 cup parsley, chopped
1 small hot red chilli, finely chopped
3 cloves garlic, chopped
3 ripe tomatoes, peeled and chopped
12 mussels in their shells, cleaned
12 cockles in their shells, cleaned
250 g fresh shrimp or prawns
250 g squid, cleaned and cut into pieces
1 cup white wine
1 tablespoon tomato paste
1 cup fish broth (see page 33) or
　　1 cup hot water and 1 fish stock cube
1 kg assorted fish fillets (gurnard, snapper, groper, blue cod, red cod, etc.), cut into cubes

Heat the oil in a large pot and sauté the onion, carrot, celery, parsley, chilli, garlic and tomatoes for a few minutes until they are tender. Add the mussels, cockles, shrimps or prawns, squid, wine, tomato paste and fish broth and bring to the boil. Add the fish cut in cubes and simmer gently until the fish is cooked. Adjust seasoning if necessary with salt and pepper.

To serve, toast a piece of bread for each person and rub it with garlic. Place it in the bottom of the soup bowl and spoon over some of the soup, making sure that there is some seafood in each bowl. Garnish with chopped parsley.

Zuppa di patate e cipolle
Potato and onion soup

This soup is much lighter than cream of potato soup but not as light as a french onion soup. It is a good soup to serve before a hearty meat stew or roast.

8–10 potatoes, peeled and cubed
1 litre beef broth (see page 33) or
   1 litre hot water and 2 teaspoons beef stock powder
50 g butter
2 tablespoons olive oil
6–8 onions, thinly sliced
$^1/_4$ cup parmesan, grated

Bring the broth to a boil and add the potato cubes. Cook for about 15 minutes or until the potatoes are tender. While the potatoes are cooking heat the oil and butter in a frying pan and gently sauté the onions until they are just beginning to turn brown.

   When the potatoes are just cooked add some of the broth to the onion pan to loosen any browned scrapings. Mash the potatoes coarsely with a potato masher, then add the onion and scrapings to the potatoes and broth and continue cooking for a few minutes. Stir the parmesan into the soup and serve in warmed bowls with extra grated parmesan on the table.

Minestra di verdure
Vegetable soup

This is like a less hearty and more refined minestrone, with the vegetables chopped up more finely.

3 cups potatoes, peeled and cubed
2 cups carrots, peeled and chopped
1 large onion, sliced
3 cloves garlic, chopped
1 cup fresh spinach, cleaned and chopped
1 stalk celery, finely chopped
$1^1/_2$ litres vegetable broth (see page 32) or
   $1^1/_2$ litres hot water and 2 teaspoons vegetable stock
   powder (e.g. Vecon)
$^1/_4$ cup tomato paste
extra virgin olive oil
2 tablespoons fresh basil, chopped or
   1 teaspoon pesto (see page 51)

Put all the ingredients except the oil and basil into a large pot and bring to a boil. Reduce the heat, cover and simmer for $1^1/_2$ hours. A few minutes before serving stir in the oil and pesto or basil and adjust the seasoning with salt and pepper if required. Serve with hunks of fresh bread.

Tortellini in brodo
Tortellini in broth

To me, this is a truly wonderful meal. The broth is light and flavourful and the tortellini are tasty and satisfying. Try using different meats for the tortellini filling if you don't fancy chicken.

2 litres chicken or beef broth or
  2 litres water and 2 teaspoons chicken or beef stock powder
1 quantity yellow pasta (see page 47)
1 spring onion, sliced

Pasta filling
100 g mortadella or ham, finely chopped
250 g cooked chicken, chopped
$^1/_4$ cup parmesan, grated
1 egg
$^1/_8$ teaspoon ground nutmeg
1 teaspoon parsley, chopped

Mix all the filling ingredients together in a bowl and set aside.

Roll the pasta into a thin sheet and cut into 5 cm squares. Place a teaspoon of the filling on each, moisten the edges and fold together into triangles. Then fold each triangle around your finger and press the two outside corners together to form what looks like a scarf over someone's head, with your finger being the head. Place on a floured board while you make the rest.

Heat the broth and, when it is boiling, drop in the tortellini and cook for 5-6 minutes until they are done.

Serve a few tortellini in each bowl with some broth and garnish with sliced spring onion.

Riso
Rice

Rice

It may surprise you to know that Italy is Europe's biggest rice producer. The rice, mainly a short-grained variety called arborio, is grown in the Piedmont and Lombardy regions. Arborio rice is particularly good for making risotto since it is able to absorb more cooking liquid than other kinds of rice and still keep its shape. Ironically, the best substitute for arborio is a long-grained or even extra-long-grained rice. These substitutes don't swell up as well but at least approximate the flavour absorption qualities of arborio rice.

A wonderfully creamy and tasty dish, risotto, which is rice cooked in a broth or sauce that is absorbed by the grains, is usually served as a first course in a traditional Italian meal. As it cooks, the rice plumps up and doesn't fall apart or clump stickily together, but remains as individual grains. Unlike rice pilaf, which is light and fluffy rice cooked in stock, risotto is heavier and creamier. It should never be either runny or dry.

Rice is also used to fortify soups, is served cold in salads, is used as fillings for vegetables or is mixed with sweet ingredients to make desserts.

Riso al burro e salvia
Rice with butter and sage leaves

This method of serving rice is also suitable for tagliatelle or ravioli.

2 cups rice
6 tablespoons parmesan, grated
100 g butter
18 fresh sage leaves

Cook the rice, set aside until required. Heat the butter and sage leaves in a pot and pour over the rice. Spoon into the serving dish and sprinkle with the cheese.

Risotto ai funghi
Rice and mushrooms

Porcini, also called ceps in France, are mushrooms that are highly praised by those in the know for their strong and pleasant flavour. You'll probably only be able to buy them dried and so they need to be soaked to release their flavour. Save the liquid they're soaked in because it's full of flavour and should be added to whatever you're making. Arborio rice is the other essential ingredient in this recipe.

$^2/_3$ cup boiling water
10 g dried porcini mushrooms
40 g butter
1 tablespoon extra virgin olive oil
1 small red onion, finely chopped
1 cup arborio rice
3 cups chicken broth (see page 34) or
   3 cups hot water and 2 chicken stock cubes

Pour the boiling water over the porcini and soak for 10 minutes. Drain, saving the liquid and cut the porcini into small pieces.

Melt the oil and butter in a pan and sauté the onion and chopped porcini until the onion is soft. Add the rice and stir to coat, about 1 minute.

Add the hot chicken stock to the rice, with the liquid in which the porcini was soaked, cover and simmer on low for about 15 minutes. Stir and continue cooking, uncovered, until all the liquid is absorbed and the rice is tender.

Risotto alla milanese
Saffron rice

Arborio rice is the best for any risotto but a long-grained rice may be substituted in an emergency. Saffron rice traditionally accompanies ossobuco (see page 81).

80 g butter
1 onion, finely chopped
1$^1/_4$ cups arborio rice
$^1/_4$ cup white wine
1 litre hot chicken broth (see page 34) or
   1 litre hot water and 2 chicken stock cubes
$^1/_2$ teaspoon ground saffron (or turmeric)
$^1/_3$ cup parmesan, grated

Melt the butter in a saucepan and sauté the onion until it is tender. Add the rice and stir together. Add the wine and cook until it is mostly absorbed. Add half of the hot broth, cover and simmer gently until it is all absorbed (about 10 minutes).

Add the remaining broth, cover and simmer until the broth is mostly absorbed and the rice is plump and tender. Stir in the saffron round about the last 5 minutes of cooking. Remove from the heat and stir in the parmesan.

Suppli
Rice croquettes

For this you need some leftover risotto (any type is fine but I prefer Risotto alla milanese). You can, of course, make some on the spot and allow it to cool, or you can make a double quantity next time and store it in the refrigerator until you're making suppli. This recipe is sometimes called suppli al telefono because the cheese in the middle stretches out like telephone wires between poles when a rice ball is broken in half. Try a different type of cheese or even pieces of ham or salami for a variation.

1 x risotto recipe (see pages 41–44), well cooled
1 egg
1 cup dried breadcrumbs
$^1/_4$ teaspoon ground nutmeg
125 g mozzarella, cut into 20–30 cubes
olive oil for frying

Scoop out about 1 tablespoon of the rice mixture, press a cube of cheese into its centre and shape into a ball. Dip the ball into the beaten egg. Mix the breadcrumbs and nutmeg and roll the balls in this mixture. Press the whole thing tightly together and place on a tray.

When all the croquettes are made, chill them for a few minutes in the freezer. Heat the oil in a pan and deep fry the suppli until they are golden all over (about 3–4 minutes). Drain on absorbent paper and serve warm.

Risotto estate
Summer-time rice

The taste of summer is brought out in this simple and delicious risotto. Make it with fresh or tinned tomatoes, fresh or dried basil, but do try it. A nice variation is to add a cube of that wonderful basil pesto (see page 51) that you made and froze in ice-cube trays during the summer when your basil plant was thick with leaves.

2 tablespoons extra virgin olive oil
2 tablespoons butter
1 medium onion, finely chopped
1 x 400 g tin tomatoes or
    400 g tomatoes, peeled
10–12 fresh basil leaves, chopped or
    2 teaspoons dried basil
$1^1/_4$ cups arborio rice
2 cups hot chicken broth (see page 34) or
    2 cups hot water and 1 chicken stock cube
$^1/_2$ cup mozzarella, grated
1 teaspoon parsley, chopped

Melt the butter and oil in a pot and sauté the onions. Purée the tomatoes in a food processor or coarsely mash with a potato masher and add to the onions. Stir in the rice and basil and cook for 5 minutes.

Pour in the hot broth and stir to mix. Cover and simmer for 15–20 minutes or until the rice is tender. Remove from the heat and stir in the mozzarella. Serve warm with a sprinkle of parsley over the rice.

Risotto di pollo
Chicken risotto

50 g butter
2 spring onions, sliced
1 small carrot, chopped
1 small stalk celery, chopped
1 cup arborio rice
3 tomatoes, peeled and chopped
1 cup white wine
2 cups hot chicken broth (see page 34) or
  2 cups hot water and 1 chicken stock cube
1 kg cooked chicken meat, chopped
$^1/_4$ cup parmesan, grated

Melt the butter in a large pot and sauté the onion, carrot and celery until they are tender. Add the rice and cook a further few minutes. Add the tomatoes and simmer 2 minutes, then add the wine and 1 cup of the broth.

Cook until the liquid is all absorbed, about 10 minutes; then add the chicken and remaining stock and cook until all this liquid is absorbed. Stir in the parmesan and serve.

Risotto di carciofi alla siciliana
Artichoke risotto

This risotto is made with small artichokes that are eaten whole, choke and all. They are usually available in smallish jars or loose from the deli section of the supermarket. I've made this recipe with roasted baby artichokes and it was particularly delicious.

2 rashers bacon
1 small onion, chopped
2 cloves garlic, chopped
2 tomatoes, peeled and chopped
1 cup arborio rice
3 cups hot vegetable broth (see page 32) or
  3 cups hot water and 2 vegetable stock cubes
1 cup baby artichoke hearts, quartered
$^1/_4$ cup parmesan or pecorino cheese, grated

Fry the bacon with a little oil from the artichokes or, if there is no oil, use 2 teaspoons of olive oil. Chop the bacon in small pieces and then add the onions, garlic and tomatoes and sauté until the vegetables are soft. Add the rice and stir together.

Add the hot broth and cook until all the liquid is absorbed, about 20 minutes. Toward the end of the cooking time stir in the quartered artichokes and cheese. Serve warm with extra grated cheese.

Risotto con cozze
Mussel risotto

This can be made with fish or vegetable broth, which should be light so that it does not overpower the flavour of the mussels.

1 kg mussels, cleaned and in the shell
50 g butter
1 onion, chopped
2 cloves garlic, chopped
1 cup arborio rice
3 cups hot fish broth (see page 33) or
   3 cups hot water and 2 fish stock cubes

Put the mussels into a pot, cover and cook until they open. Do not add water to the mussels. There will, however, be some juice left in the pot after they are all opened. This is because they hold some water within their shells. Strain this liquid to add to the broth.

   Melt the butter in a large pot and sauté the onion and garlic until tender. Add the rice and stir together, cooking for a minute. Add the mussel juice and hot fish broth and bring to the boil. Reduce the heat and simmer until the broth is all absorbed, about 20 minutes.

   Spoon the risotto into a warmed serving bowl. Then remove the top shell from the mussels and place the opened mussels decoratively among the rice.

Risotto al vino rosso
Red wine risotto

This adaptation of risotto al barolo, a risotto made with the red wine Barolo, originates from the north of Italy and is a simple and different way of serving rice.

50 g butter
2 spring onions, chopped
1 cup arborio rice
3 cups hot chicken broth (see page 34) or
   3 cups hot water and 2 chicken stock cubes
1 cup good red wine
$^{1}/_{2}$ cup parmesan, grated

Melt the butter in a large pot and sauté the onion. Stir in the rice and cook for a further minute. Add the hot chicken broth and cook until most of the stock is absorbed — about 15 minutes. Add the red wine and cook until all the wine is absorbed. Stir in the parmesan and serve immediately.

Pasta, salse e ripieni
Pasta, sauces and fillings

I have organised this chapter to give you the maximum flexibility. There are 3 different types of fresh pasta to choose from, followed by sections on sauces and fillings. With these you will be able to make any sort of pasta you like by referring to one of the recipes further on and adapting it to your choice of filling and sauce. If, for example, you wanted to make a mezzaluna-shaped pasta with a beef filling and a green sauce, then you roll and cut the pasta as indicated in the mezzaluna recipe, fill it with the beef filling on page 57 and make a sauce according to a recipe from pages 48–54. This is all absolutely acceptable and puts you in control of what you and your family like to eat.

Of course any pasta such as spaghetti, fettuccine, maccheroni or penne can simply be boiled and served with any of the sauces.

There is one thing I cannot stress too much about both dry and fresh pasta — don't overcook it. For a dried pasta such as lasagne the cooking time is 12–15 minutes; a thinner dried pasta such as spaghetti would take only 6–8 minutes. Fresh pasta is altogether different and requires only 4–5 minutes because it has so much moisture still in it. A good rule of thumb is to test the pasta after 4 minutes and continue testing it until it is done. Pasta should be al dente, that is, firm to the bite.

Pasta is served mixed with the sauce. There should be enough sauce to coat the pasta but not so much that there are pools of it left after the pasta is gone. Generally, mix the sauce and cooked pasta together in the serving dish and then sprinkle on the cheese, parsley or whatever is called for.

Pasta types

There are 2 kinds of pasta: pasta all'uovo — hand-made soft pasta meant to be used straightaway, and pasta asciutta — dried, mass-produced pasta with a long shelf life.

In northern Italy down to about Rome, pasta is generally made fresh daily. It is usually egg pasta of the ribbon type. Further south, the pasta tends to be mass-produced and dried and more of the tubular type is used.

Traditionally, certain types of pasta are used in different dishes. This is just common sense, really, since small shapes will fit on a spoon and are easier to eat in soups, whereas ribbon types are more suitable for eating with sauces.

Basic pasta recipes

Pasta gialla
Yellow pasta

3 eggs
2 cups flour

Put the eggs and flour into a food processor and whizz, stopping when you have a sticky dough. Turn onto the counter and knead, adding more flour as required. Divide the dough into 4 pieces and cover.

Use a pasta machine to roll and cut the dough or make it by hand as follows. Roll the dough until it is thin and even. Cut as required: thin narrow strips (languine) for butter and cheese; thicker wider strips (fettuccine) for meat sauces.

Cook pasta in salted boiling water for 4–6 minutes. Start timing when the water returns to the boil after the pasta has been dropped in. Stir once or twice so it doesn't stick together. This makes enough pasta for 4 people.

Pasta rosa
Pink pasta

2 eggs
2 tablespoons tomato paste
1^3/$_4$ cups flour

Put the eggs and tomato paste into a food processor and whizz, slowly adding the flour and stopping when you have a sticky dough. Turn onto the counter and knead, adding more flour as required. Divide the dough into 4 pieces and cover.

Use a pasta machine to roll and cut the dough or make it by hand as follows. Roll the dough until thin and even. Cut as required: thin narrow strips for butter and cheese; thicker wider strips for meat sauces.

Cook pasta in salted boiling water 4–6 minutes. Start timing when the water returns to the boil after the pasta has been dropped in. Stir once or twice so it doesn't stick together. This recipe makes enough pasta for 4 people.

Pasta verde
Green pasta

250 g fresh spinach
2 eggs
1 egg yolk
1³/₄ cups flour

Wash and clean the spinach leaves (do not chop) and cook them for about 4 minutes in boiling water. Drain and rinse with cold water. Squeeze out as much water as you can without losing too much of the colour.

Put the eggs, egg yolk and spinach into a food processor and whizz to chop the spinach finely. Add the flour and whizz until you have a sticky dough. Turn onto the counter and knead, adding more flour as required. Because of the spinach there is more water in this type of dough, so you may need to add quite a bit more flour to get the correct texture. Your dough should be firm but elastic and easy to roll. Divide it into 4 and cover.

Use a pasta machine to roll and cut the dough or make it by hand as follows. Roll the dough until thin and even. Cut as required: thin narrow strips for butter and cheese; thicker wider strips for meat sauces.

Cook in salted boiling water 4–6 minutes. Start timing when the water returns to the boil after the pasta has been dropped in. Stir once or twice so it doesn't stick together. This recipe makes enough pasta for 4 people.

Sauces for pasta

These are sauces for pasta, polenta and gnocchi, but they can be used wherever you need a sauce. The type of tomato you use will influence how tasty your sauce will be. The Italians mostly use San Marzano plum tomatoes or Marmande tomatoes, both of which are very flavoursome. So next time you are planting tomatoes try to get some San Marzano seeds and taste the difference.

Tinned plum tomatoes are perfectly acceptable for use in any of these sauces and fillings and for most recipes in this book which call for tomatoes.

Aglio e olio
Oil and garlic

¹/₃ cup extra virgin olive oil
3 cloves garlic, chopped
3 tablespoons parsley, chopped

Heat the oil in a pot and sauté the garlic, add the parsley and pour over the pasta. Toss lightly and serve.

Ragù alla bolognese
Bolognese sauce

A rich and tasty beef mince and tomato sauce which originates in Bologna. Don't confuse ragu with ragout, which is a stew.

Ragu is ideal with spaghetti, tagliatelle or fettuccine. It is also the standard meat sauce used in lasagne, and is ideal for serving to children, made with smaller pasta shapes, which are easier for them to eat.

3 tablespoons olive oil
1 onion, chopped
1 carrot, peeled and chopped
1 stalk celery, chopped
500 g lean beef mince
1 teaspoon beef stock powder
1 cup red wine
$^1/_4$ cup milk
400 g fresh or canned tomatoes, peeled

Heat the oil in a pan and sauté the onion, carrot and celery until tender. Add the mince and beef stock powder and sauté until barely browned. As it cooks, break up the mince with a potato masher or a fork. Add the wine and cook until the wine has evaporated. Add the milk and cook until it is all absorbed.

Add the tomatoes with their liquid. Break up the tomatoes with a potato masher as you simmer the sauce gently for an hour or more, until the meat is tender and the sauce thickened.

Salsa al pomodoro e panna
Cream and tomato sauce

This light and delicately flavoured sauce goes particularly well with a spinach-filled pasta, pasta verde or spinach gnocchi. It is also wonderful over steamed vegetables.

100 g butter
1 onion, chopped
2 x 400 g tinned tomatoes or 800 g fresh tomatoes, peeled
1 teaspoon powdered vegetable stock
$^1/_2$ cup cream

Melt the butter in a pan and sauté the onion until it is tender. Add the tomatoes with their liquid. Stir in the vegetable stock. Break up the tomatoes with a potato masher or knife and cook gently for 15 minutes.

Pour into a food processor and whizz to a smooth consistency. Return to the pan and simmer. Add the cream and cook until the sauce is warmed through. Serve immediately.

Salsa di prosciutto
Cream and ham sauce

Prosciutto ham is usually used in this recipe but you can substitute cooked ham as suggested.

220 g prosciutto or cooked ham, shredded or chopped
1 cup cream
30 g butter
$^1/_8$ teaspoon ground nutmeg
$^3/_4$ cup parmesan, grated

Combine half of the parmesan with all the other ingredients in a pot and heat through. Pour over the pasta and sprinkle with the remaining parmesan.

Salsa verde
Green sauce

A traditional sauce to go with almost everything — fish, meat, tomatoes — it keeps well in the refrigerator but must be served at room temperature to get the proper flavour.

2 cups parsley
2 tablespoons capers, drained
2 cloves garlic
3 anchovy fillets
$^1/_2$ cup extra virgin olive oil
3 tablespoons lemon juice

Put all the ingredients into a blender and blend to a thick paste.

Pesto

Pesto originated in Genoa but is now made throughout Italy. You may vary the ingredients by substituting pecorino cheese for the parmesan, or walnuts for the pine nuts, but you must always use fresh basil leaves and extra virgin olive oil.

Spoon a dollop into a bowl of soup just before serving, toss a little lightly with hot cooked pasta or use as an accompaniment to fish and meat dishes.

Pesto may be frozen for use when fresh basil is out of season. If you intend doing this, make the pesto without the cheese. Freeze it in ice-cube trays then transfer to plastic bags. Just before serving, add the cheese to the defrosted pesto. If you're eating your pesto fresh, it should be made and consumed within a day.

2 cups fresh basil leaves
3 cloves garlic
$1/2$ teaspoon salt
$2/3$ cup pine nuts
2 tablespoons parmesan, grated
1 cup extra virgin olive oil

Add half of the oil and all the other ingredients to the blender and turn it on. Slowly add the remaining oil until a thick paste is produced. This recipe makes about $2^1/2$ cups.

Pesto al basilico
Basil pesto

This is my favourite basil pesto recipe. Although it differs from the more traditional pesto recipe given opposite, I think this one allows the sweet basil flavour to sing a purer solo.

$1/4$ cup olive oil
2 cups basil leaves
$1/4$ cup pine nuts
3 tablespoons parmesan, grated

Blend together until smooth and store in a glass jar in the refrigerator until required.

Pesto di pomodori secchi
Sun-dried tomato pesto

1 cup sun-dried tomatoes
4 cloves garlic
oil from the tomatoes

Blend tomatoes and garlic with enough of the oil to make a smooth mixture. Store in glass jars until required.

Salmone e aneto
Salmon and dill sauce

This is less a sauce than a delicious combination to toss with pasta.

200 g smoked salmon (cheaper salmon offcuts are
 fine)
3 tablespoons fresh dill, finely chopped
1/4 cup extra virgin olive oil
cracked pepper

Cut the salmon into small pieces and mix with the dill and freshly ground peppers. When the pasta is cooked and drained, drizzle with the oil and toss the salmon mixture with it.

Salsa alla carbonara
Bacon and tomato sauce

4 rashers bacon, chopped
2 tablespoons olive oil
1 onion, chopped
2 cloves garlic, chopped
6 tomatoes, peeled and chopped
1 tablespoon fresh basil, chopped

Fry the bacon in the oil briefly, add the onion and garlic and sauté until transparent. Add the tomatoes and basil and simmer until the vegetables are cooked. Purée coarsely in a food processor.

Salsa d'estate
Summer sauce

6 tomatoes, peeled and chopped
1 onion, chopped
6 pitted green olives, chopped
1 tablespoon capers, drained
1/4 teaspoon dried oregano
1/3 cup parsley, chopped
2 cloves garlic, chopped
1/2 cup extra virgin olive oil

Toss all the ingredients together, cover and let stand overnight. Toss lightly with hot pasta and serve.

Tonno e funghi
Tuna and mushroom sauce

50 g butter
1 onion, chopped
100 g fresh mushrooms, sliced
185 g tuna
1¼ cups cream
2 tablespoons tomato paste
1 tablespoon parsley, chopped

Heat the butter in a pan and sauté the onion and mushrooms. Drain the tuna well and add to the mushrooms. Combine the cream and tomato paste and stir into the tuna mixture. Simmer briefly to heat through and then pour over the warm pasta, sprinkle with parsley and serve.

Salsa di pomodoro
Simple tomato sauce

800 g tomatoes, peeled and chopped
3 tablespoons olive oil
20 g butter
3 cloves garlic, chopped
salt and pepper
1 tablespoon fresh basil, chopped
1 cup parsley, chopped

Heat the oil and butter in a large pan, sauté the garlic, then add the tomatoes and gently simmer for 15 minutes. Season with salt and pepper. Add the basil and parsley, cover and simmer a further 5 minutes.

Purée in a food processor and return the mixture to the pot to simmer for a further 5 minutes. Pour over the pasta and garnish with extra parsley.

Salsa di funghi
Mushroom sauce

500 g fresh mushrooms
3 tablespoons olive oil
1 chicken stock cube
$\frac{1}{2}$ teaspoon Tabasco sauce
300 ml cream

Heat the oil in large pan and sauté the mushrooms until they begin to colour and go limp. Sprinkle in the chicken cube and add the cream and Tabasco sauce.

Reduce the heat and simmer gently for about 15 minutes or until the sauce begins to thicken. Serve warm over pasta.

Salsa Alfredo
Parmesan and cream sauce

300 ml cream
100 g parmesan, grated
salt and pepper
2 tablespoons parsley, chopped

Heat the cream in a pot then add the cheese and gently stir until melted. Remove from the heat and season with salt and pepper and parsley. Serve warm over fresh pasta.

Salsa al salmone affumicato e panna
Creamy smoked salmon sauce

A ribbon pasta such as fettuccine or tagliatelle is best with this sauce.

1 teaspoon extra virgin olive oil
3 cloves garlic, mashed
300 ml cream
250 g smoked salmon, chopped

Heat the oil in a saucepan and sauté the garlic for a minute. Add the cream, bring to the boil, then lower the heat and simmer gently for about 15 minutes until it is reduced to a slightly thicker consistency.

Stir in the salmon and pour over the warm pasta. Garnish with chopped fresh dill or parsley.

Fillings for pastas

Here are some suggestions for pasta fillings, which are all suitable for ravioli, cannelloni or cappelletti. As a general guide, these recipes make enough to fill pasta for 6 servings. It is difficult, however, to estimate how many pastas this equates to, as it depends on what type of pasta you are using, how much you put in each, how big they are and so on.

Note that the filling should not be hot as this can make the pasta soggy. Similarly, any sauce you put over uncooked pasta, such as when you assemble a lasagne, should be cool. If you're filling dried pastas such as cannelloni tubes, remember that you need to have a runnier sauce in which to cook the pasta, since a dried pasta will absorb more liquid than a fresh pasta before it is cooked.

Remember, too, that dried pasta requires longer cooking. Fresh filled pastas require only 4–5 minutes' cooking in boiling water, since they are still quite moist. Filled pasta can be frozen and will keep for several months. The smaller filled pastas can be boiled without being thawed; larger pastas such as cannelloni should be covered in a sauce and baked in the oven.

Don't forget that such ingredients as whole mussels, curly parsley or pesto can also be used as pasta fillings.

Ripieno di granchio
Crab filling

Surimi may be substituted if crab is unavailable. Sherry may be substituted for the Marsala but for the genuine Italian flavour try to use a dry Marsala.

50 g butter
2 tablespoons flour
pinch each of salt and pepper
$^3/_4$ cup milk
1 egg yolk
$^1/_4$ teaspoon Tabasco sauce
1 teaspoon lemon juice
1 tablespoon dry Marsala
250 g cooked crab meat
$^1/_4$ cup dried breadcrumbs

Make a white sauce by melting the butter in a saucepan and stirring in the flour and salt and pepper. Let this mixture bubble and brown slightly, stirring occasionally so it doesn't burn (about 1 minute). Pour in the milk and stir until the sauce thickens.

Remove from the heat and beat in the egg yolk. Stir in the Tabasco, lemon juice and Marsala, then mix in the crab and breadcrumbs. When cooled, this is ready to fill your pasta.

Ripieno di prosciutto, spinaci e funghi
Ham, spinach and mushroom filling

You may substitute ham for the prosciutto if the latter is hard to get.

1 cup cooked spinach, finely chopped
100 g prosciutto or ham, finely chopped
1 egg, beaten
3 tablespoons parmesan, grated
1 cup fresh mushrooms, chopped

Mix all the ingredients together.

Ripieno di prosciutto e funghi
Ham and mushroom filling

You can vary this by the type of mushrooms you use.

30 g butter
1^1/$_2$ cups fresh mushrooms, chopped
salt and pepper
^{1}/$_2$ cup ham, chopped
^{1}/$_2$ cup parmesan or pecorino, grated
1 egg
^{1}/$_4$ cup parsley, chopped
2 tablespoons cream

Melt the butter in a frying pan and sauté the mushrooms until tender, about 5 minutes. Remove from the heat, mix with all the remaining ingredients and allow to cool before using.

Ripieno di spinaci e ricotta
Spinach and ricotta filling

This Northern Italian recipe is particularly suitable for a closed pasta such as ravioli or tortellini. You may substitute cream cheese or cottage cheese for the ricotta.

500 g spinach, cleaned and trimmed
1 tablespoon olive oil
1 small onion, chopped
$1/4$ teaspoon ground nutmeg
$1^1/4$ cups ricotta cheese
1 egg, beaten

Bring a pot of water to the boil and add the spinach. Bring it to the boil again and then drain well. Squeeze out as much water as you can and chop the spinach coarsely.

Heat the oil in a pan and sauté the onion. Mix the spinach, sautéed onion, nutmeg and ricotta and combine well. Remove from the heat and allow to cool slightly before stirring in the beaten egg. Refrigerate until required.

Ripieno alla bolognese
Bolognese beef mince filling

2 tablespoons olive oil
1 onion, chopped
4 cloves garlic, chopped
500 g lean beef mince
2 tablespoons red wine
$1/4$ cup tomato paste
1 tablespoon oregano, fresh or dried
$1/4$ cup parmesan, grated
3 tablespoons dried breadcrumbs
1 tablespoon stock powder
salt and pepper

Heat the oil in a saucepan and sauté the onion and garlic until tender (about 2 minutes). Add the beef mince and fry until brown all over. Add the red wine, then the tomato paste and oregano, and stir together to mix.

Remove from the heat, stir in the parmesan and breadcrumbs and sprinkle with beef stock powder. Adjust the seasoning with salt and pepper if required.

Ripieno di pesce
Fish filling

A light and delicate filling suitable for closed pasta such as anolini, which will be cooked in a broth and served as a soup. You can substitute cottage cheese for the ricotta.

500 g skinned and boned fish, e.g. sole, gurnard or
   snapper
¹/₂ cup white wine
1 onion, sliced
5 sprigs parsley
water to cover
¹/₄ cup ricotta cheese
2 tablespoons parsley, chopped
salt and pepper

Lay the sliced onion in a high-sided saucepan which is just big enough to hold the fish. Put the fillets on top of the onion and place the parsley sprigs over the fish. Pour in the wine and add just enough water to cover.

Bring to the boil, then simmer gently until the fish is cooked, about 10-15 minutes. Drain the fish and discard the vegetables and liquid.

Mash the fish, ricotta and chopped parsley into a coarse mixture. Adjust the seasoning with salt and pepper if required.

Pasta dishes

The following recipes are general suggestions for dishes made with pasta, sauces and fillings. Feel free to substitute alternative pastas, sauces or fillings — experiment!

Pasta al burro e formaggio
Pasta with butter and cheese

This is the simplest and most common way of eating pasta in Italy. Any pasta type, filled or unfilled, small shapes or ribbons, can be cooked in this way.

1 quantity fresh (see pages 47–48) or
   dried pasta of your choice
100 g butter
¹/₂ cup parmesan, grated

Bring a pot of salted water to the boil and cook the pasta according to instructions. While the pasta is cooking melt the butter.

Drain the pasta well and toss in a large warm bowl with the melted butter. Sprinkle the parmesan over and toss lightly together. Serve hot with extra parmesan in a bowl on the side.

Fusilli con spinaci
Fusilli with spinach

Fusilli are small spiral pasta, but any type of small pasta would be suitable for this dish.

250 g spinach, washed and chopped
3 tablespoons extra virgin olive oil
4 cloves garlic, crushed
6 anchovy fillets, chopped
$^1/_2$ teaspoon ground chilli powder
2 cups uncooked fusilli

Bring 2 litres of water to the boil with 1 teaspoon salt, add the spinach and cook for 2 minutes after the water has returned to the boil. Remove the spinach and squeeze out as much water as possible.

Retain the boiling water and cook the fusilli in it according to the directions on the package.

Heat the oil in a frying pan, sauté the garlic and anchovies for about 30 seconds, then add the spinach and chilli powder. Toss lightly together and cook just long enough to heat all the ingredients through.

Serve immediately over the drained cooked pasta and garnish with grated parmesan or pecorino.

Fettuccine con spinaci e funghi
Fettuccine with spinach and mushrooms

The porcini mushrooms add that extra dimension to this dish. They are quite expensive but well worth it. If you don't have porcini then use 100 g of good quality, tasty field mushrooms instead. Fresh mushrooms will not need to be soaked.

20 g dried porcini
250 g fresh spinach or silverbeet
100 g butter
250 g dried spaghetti
$^1/_4$ cup cream
$^1/_4$ cup parmesan, grated
200 g dried fettuccine

Soak the porcini for 15 minutes in just enough warm water to cover. Chop finely.

Put the water in which the porcini were soaked in a larger pot and add enough extra water to cook the pasta. Bring the water to a boil and cook the pasta according to the instructions on the packet.

Parboil the spinach in boiling water for 2 minutes. Drain well, squeeze out as much water as you can and chop finely. Melt the butter in a frying pan and sauté the spinach for 5 minutes.

Stir in the porcini and cream and cook a further 2 minutes. Spoon into a serving bowl, sprinkle with the parmesan and toss lightly together. Serve warm.

Cappelletti di ricotta e spinaci
Cappelletti filled with ricotta and spinach

Serving cappelletti (little hats) in this traditionally easy way means you don't have to make a sauce. You do, however, need to use the best quality parmesan and ricotta available.

1 x quantity spinach and ricotta filling (see page 57)
1 x quantity pasta gialla (see page 47)
100 g butter
¹/₂ cup parmesan, grated

Roll out the pasta into a sheet and cut out circles about 6-8 cm diameter. Place a teaspoon of filling into each, moisten the edges with water and press together to form a semi-circle. Fold the points of the semi-circle around your finger and squeeze together to form a little hat-like shape. Set aside until you have made them all.

Bring a large pot of water to the boil and add the cappelletti. When the water returns to the boil, time for 5 minutes. The pasta should be cooked but taste-test it to make sure.

Drain the pasta well and spoon onto a warmed serving plate. Pour over the butter and sprinkle with the grated parmesan.

Cannelloni
Meat-stuffed cannelloni

Cannelloni are large tubes of pasta stuffed with a tasty meat filling and covered with a delicious tomato sauce. You can buy dried cannelloni tubes at a supermarket or grocery store. These need to be parboiled briefly beforehand.

You can fill cannelloni with a range of stuffings including chicken, fish and vegetables, and bake them according to this recipe. See pages 55–58 for suggestions.

12 large cannelloni tubes
1 quantity bolognese filling (page 57)
250 g ricotta (or cottage) cheese
1 quantity simple tomato sauce (page 53)
1 cup parmesan, grated

Bring a pot of salted water to the boil and cook the cannelloni tubes for 2 minutes. Remove and drain well on a wet teatowel.

Mix the ricotta with the bolognese filling once it has cooled. Fill the tubes. An easy way to do this is by spooning the mixture into a piping bag without a nozzle and squeezing it into the tubes. Otherwise simply spoon the mixture into the tubes.

Place the filled tubes in a lightly oiled casserole dish, packing them tightly together, and cover with the warm tomato sauce. Sprinkle with parmesan and bake at 200°C for 15 minutes or until golden.

Lasagne alla bolognese
Lasagne

Lasagne is a casserole made with a beef and tomato sauce (bolognese sauce), layered with cheese and pasta. I do hope you will make your own sheets of pasta for this most delicious and popular dish. Always allow the lasagne to cool for at least 10 minutes after taking out of the oven, so that it doesn't fall apart when you serve it. If you want to present it in neat squares, then cook it a day before it is required and store it, covered, in the refrigerator. You will find it much easier to cut into neat shapes while cold, and you can easily reheat it in the microwave or oven.

1 tablespoon olive oil
1 large onion, chopped
4 cloves garlic, chopped
250 g fresh mushrooms, chopped
500 g lean beef mince
1 teaspoon dried oregano
500 g fresh or tinned tomatoes, peeled
$1/_2$ cup red wine
3 tablespoons tomato paste
1 cup beef broth (see page 33) or
   1 cup hot water and 1 beef stock cube
250 g ricotta cheese (or cottage cheese)
300 g parmesan, grated
$1/_2$ quantity pasta (see pages 47–48) in 2 sheets or
   200 g dried lasagne pasta
2 tablespoons parsley, chopped

Heat the oil in a pan and sauté the onion, garlic and mushrooms until they are tender. Add the beef and brown well. Sprinkle with the oregano and add the tomatoes, red wine, tomato paste and beef broth.

Break up the mince and tomatoes with a potato masher or, for a finer texture, whizz the meat sauce briefly in the food processor.

Simmer gently for about 15 minutes or until the sauce thickens slightly. Remove from the heat and cool a little.

To assemble the lasagne, spoon about a third of the sauce into the bottom of a casserole dish (about 30 x 15 cm) and place a sheet of pasta over all the sauce. Spread the ricotta over it in spoonfuls and top with another third of the sauce. Place the second sheet of pasta over that and spoon over the remaining sauce.

Sprinkle the grated parmesan over the top and bake at 150°C for about 1 hour. Remove from the oven, garnish with the parsley and remember to allow to sit for 10 minutes before serving.

Ravioli e pollo
Ravioli with chicken filling

1 quantity pasta gialla (see page 47)
1 quantity simple tomato sauce (see page 53)

Filling
2 cups cooked chicken, chopped
4 rashers bacon
3 cloves garlic, mashed
¹/₄ cup parsley, chopped
3 tablespoons cream
2 tablespoons parsley, chopped
¹/₄ cup parmesan, grated

Fry the bacon, remove from the pan and chop into small pieces. Add the mashed garlic to the bacon fat in the pan and sauté briefly.

Remove from the heat and add the chicken, bacon, ¹/₄ cup of parsley and cream. Stir together and set aside to cool.

Cut the pasta dough into 2 equal-sized pieces. Roll out 1 piece into a sheet and place teaspoonfuls of filling 4 cm apart on it. Brush a little water between the mounds of filling. Roll out the second half of the dough and place it over the first. Press between the rows and columns to seal the sheets together and form squares. Cut the squares out with a pastry-cutter or sharp knife. Make sure the edges are well sealed.

Bring a large pot of water to the boil and add half of the ravioli. When the water returns to the boil, time for 5–10 minutes. Test a ravioli to make sure it is cooked and then drain the rest well in a colander. Keep warm while you cook the second lot. Put the ravioli into a warmed serving bowl.

Heat the tomato sauce and pour over the ravioli, toss together lightly and sprinkle with the 2 tablespoons of chopped parsley and the parmesan.

Tortellini di zucca
Tortellini filled with pumpkin

The sage butter adds a wonderful nutty herb flavour which complements the pumpkin well.

Filling
500 g prepared pumpkin purée (see below)
¹/₂ cup parmesan, grated
¹/₂ cup ground almonds
¹/₄ teaspoon ground nutmeg

1 quantity pasta gialla (see page 47)
100 g butter
10–12 fresh sage leaves
¹/₂ cup parmesan, grated

Pumpkin purée
750 g pumpkin, cut into pieces and de-seeded

Bake the pumpkin in the oven at 180°C for about 30 minutes.

Scrape the flesh off the skin and purée it in a food processor. Next make the filling by mixing all the ingredients together.

Roll out the pasta into sheets and cut into circles about 5 cm in diameter. Place a teaspoon of the pumpkin filling on each and fold in half. Seal the edges well and then wrap the ends around your finger and squeeze together to form a little hat-like shape.

Bring a pot of salted water to the boil and add half of the tortellini. When the water returns to the boil, time for 4–5 minutes. Test that the pasta is cooked and drain. Keep warm while you cook the remaining tortellini.

Heat the butter and add the sage leaves. Cook briefly until the butter just begins to brown. Remove from the heat and pour over the warm tortellini in a serving bowl. Sprinkle with the grated parmesan and serve.

Fettuccine con salsa al limone
Fettuccine and lemon sauce

This delicate sauce goes well with any plain pasta. Grappa is a strong Italian brandy. If you don't have a bottle on hand, you can use ordinary brandy or cognac instead.

1 quantity pasta (see pages 47-48) cut into
   fettuccine or 500 g dried fettuccine
300 ml cream
1 grated lemon rind
juice of 1 lemon
3 tablespoons grappa
ground nutmeg

Bring a large pot of salted water to the boil and cook the pasta. Use the instructions given, but undercook slightly for this recipe.

Make the sauce by pouring the cream into a pot with the grated lemon rind and bringing to the boil. Reduce the heat and simmer gently for 5 minutes. Stir in the lemon juice and grappa.

Drain the pasta well and add to the sauce and continue cooking a further 5 minutes or until the sauce thickens. Serve hot with a sprinkle of ground nutmeg.

Mezzaluna agli spinaci alla parmigiana
Spinach-filled mezzaluna with parmesan

Mezzaluna or filled semi-circles are perhaps the easiest pasta to fill.

1 quantity pasta gialla (see page 47)
1 quantity spinach and ricotta filling (see page 57)
1 quantity parmesan and cream sauce (see page 54)
Italian parsley

Roll out the dough and cut into round pieces 5 cm in diameter. Place half a teaspoonful of the filling on each circle and fold it in half. Press the edges together to seal and place on a floured board until all the mezzaluna are made.

Bring a pot of salted water to the boil and drop in half of the mezzaluna. When the water returns to the boil time it for 4 minutes and then remove the pasta to a colander to drain while you make the remaining pasta.

Heat the sauce and pour over the hot cooked mezzaluna in a warmed serving bowl. Garnish with chopped Italian parsley.

Conchiglie e zucchini
Seashell pasta with zucchini

This dish consists of a cheese sauce tossed together with diced zucchini and seashell pasta. It is not too heavy a meal and a tasty way of using up your garden's over-production of zucchini.

50 g butter
1 tablespoon flour
milk
salt and pepper
2 tablespoons fresh basil, chopped
$1/_4$ cup parmesan, grated
3 zucchini, diced
$1/_4$ cup olive oil
500 g dried seashell pasta

Melt the butter in a frying pan, stir the flour into the butter and cook until it begins to turn brown. Stir in the milk, a little at a time, to make a smooth sauce. Season and stir in the chopped basil and parmesan. Cook gently for a few minutes until the cheese is all melted and the sauce is smooth.

Cut the zucchini into 1 cm slices then cut each of these into 4. Heat the oil in a frying pan and sauté the zucchini so that it is brown on all sides. Drain on absorbent paper, put into the cheese sauce and stir to coat. Keep warm.

Bring a pot of salted water to the boil and cook the pasta according to the directions on the packet. Drain well and toss together with the zucchini in the sauce.

Pesce
Fish

The Italians' way with fish is very much in keeping with their overall philosophy on food: not to overcook, overseason or oversauce. Fish must, of course, be fresh and this is why, in Italy, you are unlikely to find fish dishes served very far from the coast.

There are 5 main ways of cooking fish. All require minimal cooking and use very few other ingredients to enhance the fish's natural flavour and texture. A wonderful, easy and tasty way of serving fish is to pan fry it and serve it with a bowl of Italian mayonnaise or green sauce (see page 50).

You can grill fish (alla griglia) in the oven; this particularly suits the more oily fish since grilling drives off much of the oil when it might leave leaner fish dry. Marinating fish fillets in lemon juice, herbs and olive oil and then grilling adds a subtle flavour and allows you to grill fish that would otherwise be too lean. Shellfish, too, cook up well when grilled.

Fish can also be fried in a pan (in padella) with a mixture of oil and butter. This is particularly suitable for small whole fish such as flounder, sole, trout or salmon. Fish fillets and processed fish such as fishballs are often done in this way.

Fish can be poached (in bianco) in either seasoned water, wine or stock. This suits both small and larger whole fish, which can then be beautifully presented.

The technique of cooking fish wrapped in foil or leaves (al cartoccio) is an impressive and very easy way of cooking all types of fish and shellfish. It allows them to retain much of their own juices and flavour.

And finally you can bake (al forno) fish. This is mostly done with large whole fish, which may also be stuffed.

Maionese
Italian mayonnaise

This mayonnaise is a creamy chartreuse colour because of the yellow egg yolks and green extra virgin olive oil. It is generally served in a bowl alongside a dish, rather than dolloped on top of the food or mixed into it. It is particularly fine with seafood but goes well with vegetables too.

1 cup extra virgin olive oil
3 egg yolks
$1/_2$ teaspoon salt
1 tablespoon lemon juice

Put the egg yolks, salt, lemon juice and half of the oil into a blender and turn it on. While it is running slowly pour in the remaining oil. This should take about 30 seconds from start to finish. Mayonnaise will keep for 3 weeks in a jar in the refrigerator.

Pesce al pomodoro
Fishballs with tomato sauce

This very simple fishball recipe can be dressed up with other sauces, such as salsa verde or maionese.

250 g fish fillets
1 cup dried breadcrumbs
1 cup parsley, chopped
250 g fresh or canned tomatoes, peeled
1 cup water
salt and pepper

Purée the first 3 ingredients in a food processor and season with salt and pepper. Roll into balls and fry in olive oil until golden. Remove and keep warm.

Simmer the tomatoes and 1 cup water in a saucepan until the tomatoes are soft. Then purée them in a food processor, return them to the saucepan and continue cooking until the sauce begins to thicken, about 30 minutes.

Serve the fishballs on a bed of cooked pasta with sauce poured over and garnished with some chopped parsley.

Tranci di salmone al forno
Baked salmon steaks

A layer of seasoned breadcrumbs over the steaks protects them from drying out and at the same time soaks up some of the oil and juices to make a crisp and delicate crust.

4–6 thick salmon steaks
olive oil
salt and pepper to taste
1 cup dried breadcrumbs
1 clove garlic, mashed
1 tablespoon parsley, finely chopped
1–2 anchovy fillets, finely chopped
1 tablespoon capers, drained and chopped

Pre-heat the oven to 200°C. Lightly oil a baking dish with the olive oil and place fish inside, in a single layer. Sprinkle with salt and pepper, and drizzle with a little more of the oil.

Mix the breadcrumbs, garlic, parsley, anchovy and capers together either by hand or whizz briefly in a food processor for a more finely textured topping. Sprinkle this over the salmon steaks and drizzle with a little of the olive oil.

Bake for 10–15 minutes or until the steaks are cooked. Do not overcook! Serve with wedges of fresh lemon.

Pesce al forno
Baked whole fish

This is a great way of cooking any whole large fish such as snapper, trumpeter, groper, bluenose or warehou. Dried oregano and rosemary may be used instead of fresh. You must use fresh parsley.

2 kg whole fish, cleaned and scaled
8–10 large sprigs parsley
$\frac{1}{2}$ cup olive oil
1 teaspoon fresh oregano, chopped
2 cloves garlic, crushed
1 teaspoon fresh rosemary
salt and pepper
1 tablespoon lemon juice
$\frac{1}{4}$ cup tomato purée
1 cup water
$\frac{1}{2}$ cup black olives

Pre-heat the oven to 200°C. Oil a baking dish large enough to hold the fish with about half of the olive oil. Sprinkle in the oregano and lay the parsley over the bottom and sides of the dish.

Rub the inside of the fish with the garlic, rosemary, salt and pepper. Place the fish on top of the parsley in the prepared baking dish. Place the olives around the fish.

Mix the lemon juice, tomato purée and water and pour over the fish. Cover with foil and bake for 30 minutes. Remove the foil, baste the fish and continue baking until the fish is done. This will depend on the size and thickness of the fish but should take about 15 minutes once uncovered. Baste the fish several times once the foil is removed. Serve directly from the baking dish.

Pesce in bianco con salsa verde
Poached fish with green sauce

This recipe can be used equally well for any type of fish fillet. Vary the sauce used to suit your requirements. See sauces on pages 48–54 for ideas.

4–6 fish fillets, skinned and boned
1 teaspoon salt
$\frac{1}{4}$ cup salsa verde (page 50)
1 lemon

Place the fillets in a frying pan with just enough water to cover them. Sprinkle with the salt, squeeze half of the lemon into the water, cover and bring to the boil.

From the time it comes to the boil, time for 3–4 minutes, depending on how thick the fillets are, and then remove to a warmed plate to drain for about 3 minutes. Pour away any liquid that comes off the fish.

Have the salsa verde at room temperature and spoon some of it over each fillet. Serve with lemon wedges.

Pesce ripieno
Stuffed and baked whole fish

The tricky part with this recipe is removing the guts, backbone and rib bones from the back of the fish. Don't cut right through the belly but instead leave a pouch for the stuffing, with the fish sitting on its stomach and the top open with the stuffing. For best results use Italian parsley.

2 kg whole fish, cleaned and scaled as indicated above
2 onions, sliced in rings
5 sprigs parsley
salt and pepper
$^1/_2$ cup fish broth (see page 33) or
  $^1/_2$ cup white wine

Stuffing
2 tablespoons olive oil
100 g mushrooms, cleaned and chopped
2 tender celery stalks, finely chopped
1 cup dried breadcrumbs
1 teaspoon parsley, chopped
2 tablespoons fish broth (see page 33) or
  2 tablespoons white wine

Pre-heat the oven to 220°C. Lightly oil a baking dish large enough to hold the fish. Lay the onion rings in the dish and place the parsley sprigs over that. Rub the inside of the fish with salt and pepper.

To make the stuffing, heat the oil and sauté the mushrooms and celery until they are limp. Remove from the heat and stir in the breadcrumbs, parsley and 2 tablespoons of fish broth or wine as you choose. Mix well and spoon into the fish.

Place the fish on top of the onion rings and pour in the $^1/_2$ cup of fish broth or wine. Cover the stuffing part of the fish only with foil and bake for 20-25 minutes or until the fish is cooked. Serve with onion rings from the pan and lemon wedges. Beware of the odd bone still left in the fish!

Pesce alla griglia
Grilled fish

The fillets and steaks of most fish types are suitable for this recipe. I often use salmon, kingfish or groper. The steaks should be about 3 cm thick so if you are using a thinner fillet be sure to adjust the cooking time accordingly.

4–6 thick fish steaks, about 3 cm
50 g butter, at room temperature
$\frac{1}{4}$ cup parsley, chopped

Preheat the grill so that the steaks can go under a hot grill immediately.

Mix the butter and parsley together. Place the steaks on a rack in a baking tray and spread each with the parsley butter, using about half of it.

Grill for 4 minutes, then remove from the grill, turn the steaks and spread with the remaining parsley butter. Return to the grill and finish the cooking by grilling for a further 2–3 minutes.

Serve with lemon wedges and a sprinkle of salt if required.

Salmonata con riso e gamberi in bianco
Poached salmon with rice and shrimp

This is suitable for any small whole fish. Here I use 4 salmon, one for each dinner guest. For more guests, simply add extra salmon and increase the cooking time slightly. Serves 4.

1 small onion, sliced
1 carrot, cut in quarters
2 sprigs parsley
1 stalk celery, coarsely chopped
3 cloves garlic, chopped
1 cup dry white wine
2 teaspoons salt
$\frac{1}{4}$ teaspoon pepper
4 x 250 g baby salmon
2 tablespoons extra virgin olive oil
2 cups uncooked rice
1 spring onion, thinly sliced into rings
4 cups fish broth (see page 33) or 4 cups hot water
    and 3 teaspoons fish stock powder
2 tablespoons extra virgin olive oil
1 kg cooked shrimp
10–12 whole black olives

Put 3–4 cups of water in a frying pan and add the onion, carrot, parsley, celery, garlic, wine, salt and pepper. Cover and bring to the boil, reduce the heat and simmer for 30 minutes. Place the fish in the hot poaching liquid and bring to the boil again, reduce the heat and simmer for 25 minutes.

While the fish is poaching prepare the rice by heating the oil in a pot and adding the rice and spring onions, stirring to coat all over with oil. Add the hot fish stock, cover and bring to a boil, reduce heat and simmer for 15–18 minutes until rice is done.

Heat the 2 tablespoons extra virgin olive oil and sauté the shrimps to heat them through.

When the fish is cooked place it on a serving platter with the rice around the edge and the shrimps and olives placed decoratively around and among it.

Pellegrine alla fiorentina
Florentine style scallops

This may be served in a single, shallow, large casserole dish or in small individual ramekins. For a change you can substitute raw mussels or even squid rings for the scallops.

800 g fresh spinach
25 g salted butter
$^{1}/_{4}$ teaspoon ground nutmeg
6–8 medium potatoes, peeled and quartered
30 g butter
pinch of pepper
2 tablespoons parmesan, grated
milk
1 kg scallops, shelled
2 teaspoons extra virgin olive oil
20 g butter
2 cloves garlic, crushed
$^{1}/_{2}$ cup dry white wine
300 ml cream
$^{1}/_{2}$ cup parmesan, grated
2 tablespoons parsley, chopped

Clean the spinach and discard any stalks. Parboil in boiling salted water for 2 minutes. Drain and squeeze out as much of the liquid as you can; chop coarsely. Melt the butter in a saucepan, add the spinach and sprinkle with nutmeg. Toss together to coat the spinach.

Boil the potatoes in salted water until they are cooked. Drain well and mash in a food mixer (not a processor or blender) or by hand with the butter, pepper, parmesan and enough milk to make a smooth, firm mixture.

Heat the oil and butter in a large frying pan and add the well-drained scallops, garlic and wine. Cover and bring to the boil and cook for 4 minutes.

Pre-heat the oven to 220°C. Spoon the spinach into a shallow baking dish. Using a slotted spoon, scoop out the scallops and arrange them on top of the spinach in the centre of the dish. Spoon the mashed potatoes into a bag and pipe around the inside edge of the baking dish on top of the spinach.

Add the cream to the poaching liquid and simmer to reduce and thicken the sauce, about 15 minutes. Pour this sauce over the scallops, sprinkle with the parmcsan and bake for 5 minutes or until the parmesan is golden and the whole thing is warmed through. Remove from the oven and sprinkle with the parsley. Allow to cool slightly before serving.

Pesce al forno con patate
Fish baked with potatoes

This casserole of thinly sliced potatoes with fish and mussels, which are seasoned with chilli and herbs, is similar to a fish dish made in the Apulian area. I suggest smoked snapper, kingfish, trout or kahawai as ideal smoked fish to use. Do not use kippered fish of any kind. The fresh and smoked fish you use should be of the same type.

1.5 kg mussels in the shell
1 cup white wine
1 lemon, sliced
5 cloves garlic, peeled
2 kg potatoes
2 x 400 g tins tomatoes, peeled
$^{1}/_{2}$ cup parsley, chopped
2 teaspoons chilli powder
1 cup parmesan or pecorino, grated
pinch fennel seeds
8 cloves garlic, chopped
500 g smoked fish
1 kg fresh fish fillets, skinned and boned

Put the mussels, wine, lemon slices and 5 garlic cloves into a large pot, cover and bring to the boil. Cook for about 3 minutes or until the mussels open. Remove from their shells and set aside. Strain the solid particles from the liquid.

Peel the potatoes, slice very thinly and soak the slices in cold water until required. Drain and pat them dry. Drain the tomatoes and cut them into slices; allow the liquid to drain away.

Mix the parsley, chilli powder, parmesan, fennel seeds and chopped garlic.

Lightly oil a large casserole dish and place in it a layer of half of the potatoes. Lay half of the sliced tomatoes over them and then sprinkle over these a third of the cheese mixture. The next layer is made up of the smoked fish, fresh fish and mussels mixed together.

Sprinkle half of the remaining cheese mixture over the fish and spoon over half of the mussel liquid. Lay the remaining tomatoes over the fish layer, then the remaining cheese mixture and sprinkle with the remaining mussel liquid. Drizzle the oil over the whole thing and cover with a lid of foil.

Bake in a pre-heated oven at 200°C for 40 minutes. After 20 minutes' cooking remove the foil and continue cooking. Test that the potatoes are cooked and remove from the oven. Allow to cool for about 10 minutes before serving.

Fish

Cozze all'Italiana
Italian style mussels

1 loaf french bread
1.5 kg mussels in the shell
1 tablespoon olive oil
1 onion, chopped
$^1/_2$ cup parsley, chopped
3 cloves garlic, chopped
1 cup dry white wine
parsley, chopped

Heat the oil in a large frying pan and sauté the onions, $^1/_2$ cup of parsley and garlic. Add the white wine and bring to the boil, then add the mussels in their shells. Cover and bring back to the boil. Reduce the heat and cook until the mussels have opened – about 5 minutes.

In the meantime cut the bread into thick rounds and place on a baking sheet. Brush with a little olive oil and bake in the oven at 200°C for 5–10 minutes or until they are slightly toasted and warm. Keep them warm in the oven until required.

To serve, put a slice or two of the bread into each bowl and spoon over some mussels and liquid. Garnish with chopped parsley and serve while hot.

Salmone con pancetta
Salmon with bacon

Other small whole fish such as blue cod or trout are also good in this recipe. Serves 4.

4 pan-sized salmon, about 250 g each
8 rashers streaky bacon
4 tablespoons olive oil
3 cloves garlic, chopped
1 cup vegetable broth (see page 32) or
  1 cup hot water and 1 teaspoon vegetable stock
  powder
3 tablespoons tomato purée
2 tablespoons fresh basil, chopped, or
  1 tablespoon basil pesto (see page 51)
2 tablespoons capers

Clean and scale the salmon. Wrap each fish in 2 rashers of bacon and gently fry in the oil. Brown on both sides and then place in a casserole dish.

Sauté the garlic briefly in the oil and then add the tomato purée, broth and basil and simmer gently for about 5 minutes.

Spoon the sauce over the fish and bake at 180°C for 15–20 minutes. Sprinkle with the capers and serve.

Calamari con ripieno di prezzemolo
Parsley-stuffed squid

This is a recipe for parsley-stuffed squid in a spicy tomato sauce. Squid is quite easy to deal with, although it is a bit messy to clean. If you don't want to go to the bother, then buy cleaned squid tubes from the fish shop and get an extra one instead of the tentacles to make the stuffing.

6 whole squid about 12 cm long or
   10 cleaned squid tubes about 12 cm long
3 anchovy fillets, finely chopped
3 tablespoons parsley, chopped
3 cloves garlic, sliced
1/4 cup parmesan, grated
3/4 cup dried breadcrumbs
2 tablespoons extra virgin olive oil
1 egg, beaten
3 tablespoons extra virgin olive oil
400 g fresh or canned tomatoes, peeled and chopped
1 small red chilli, chopped
1 cup white wine

Clean the squid, retaining only the tubes and tentacles. Chop the tentacles (or the extra squid tube) into small pieces and mix with the anchovy, parsley, garlic, parmesan, breadcrumbs, oil and beaten egg. Spoon the filling into 6 squid tubes so that they are each half filled.

Heat the oil in a frying pan just large enough to hold the squid tubes and sauté the tomatoes. Add the chilli and wine and whizz briefly in the food processor. Return the sauce to the pan and lay the stuffed squid in the sauce. Cover and simmer for about 30 minutes. Serve hot over rice.

Filetti di pesce passera con salsa di capperi e pomodoro
Flounder with caper and tomato sauce

1 quantity simple tomato sauce (page 53)
3 tablespoons capers, well drained and chopped
10–12 flounder fillets (about 1 kg total)

Make the sauce according to the instructions on page 53. After the sauce has been puréed and returned to the pan to simmer, add the well-drained capers and continue cooking for a further 5 minutes.

Spoon a third of the sauce into a casserole dish just large enough to hold the fish. Fold the fish in half, skin side in, and place in a row along the centre of the casserole dish. Pour on the remaining sauce and bake in the oven at 230°C for 5 minutes or until the fish is cooked. Don't overcook it!

Remove the fish to a warm serving platter and keep warm while you reduce the sauce further. Boil the sauce to reduce it to a thicker consistency. Pour the sauce over the fish and serve while hot.

Carne e pollo
Meat and chicken

Think of meat in an Italian context and veal should come to mind first. It is, however, quite expensive both here and in Italy and so is used only for special occasions. This meat comes in 2 forms, depending on its age. Vitello is from milk-fed calves killed at about 3 weeks, before they have ever eaten grass. Many non-Italians find milk-fed veal rather lacking in flavour and the texture dull. Vitellone, which comes from older animals that have had the opportunity to eat grass, is richer in colour, firmer in texture and has more flavour.

Beef, too, is pretty expensive in Italy but here in New Zealand it is generally a more affordable meat. Beef comes from a bullock (manzo), not from a cow (mucca), and should be lean. Sometimes it is marinated before cooking and then served with the same type of wine in which it was marinated. Beef fillet is often grilled and served with a simple sauce or butter.

Pork, another Italian favourite, is used in many different forms from prosciutto to whole suckling pigs. In fact, in one form or another, pork is the most commonly used meat in Italy.

Lamb is extremely tasty and versatile and is used in many Italian dishes. A rather nice combination of lamb and rabbit roasted together is popular in the south and shows the simplicity and ingenuity for which Italian cooking is famous.

Chicken is cooked in many ways but spit roasting is probably the most popular. The mouth-watering aroma of a chicken cooking on a rotisserie is wonderful and will guarantee to bring the family to the dinner table on time. Not only is chicken considered better for us than other more fatty meats, but it is also quick and simple to cook in a wide variety of ways, is cheap and easy to buy and tastes absolutely delicious!

Filetto alla grappa
Beef fillet and grappa

Brandy or cognac can be substituted for the grappa. You may also use a different top quality cut of meat such as scotch fillet, tenderloin or rib-eye steak. Serves 4.

4 fillet steaks
50 g butter
$1/4$ teaspoon rosemary, chopped
3 tablespoons grappa
3 tablespoons Worcestershire sauce
1 teaspoon prepared mild mustard

Melt the butter in a frying pan and sprinkle in the rosemary. Immediately place the steaks on top of the rosemary and fry for 2 minutes.

Mix the grappa, Worcestershire sauce and mustard together. Turn the steak and fry for 1 minute then add the grappa mixture and cook for 1 more minute.

Remove the meat and keep warm. Bring the sauce to the boil, strain and pour a little sauce over each steak.

Bistecca alla fiorentina
Florentine grilled steak

As its name suggests, this method of simply grilling a steak originated in Florence. Use very good quality steak, sirloin, T-bone or rump steak. Put only a few drops of oil on the steak after it has been grilled. Steak cooked this way should be very rare.

A good cut of venison is excellent done this way. Serves 4.

4 sirloin steaks
2 teaspoons cracked peppercorns
salt
extra virgin olive oil

Sprinkle the peppercorns onto both sides of the steaks. Pre-heat the grill to high. Place the meat on a wire rack over a roasting tray and grill close to the element for 4 minutes.

Turn and grill a further 4 minutes or until it is cooked to the degree you like. Remove from the griller and brush with a little oil. Serve at once.

Coda alla vaccinara
Oxtail ragout

Oxtail requires long, slow cooking to soften it and allow its flavours to mingle with the other ingredients. This dish is both very simple and very tasty.

2 kg oxtail
1 carrot, coarsely chopped
1 celery stalk, coarsely chopped
1 onion, coarsely chopped
2 tablespoons olive oil
1 teaspoon parsley
1 carrot, finely chopped
1 celery stalk, finely chopped
2 bay leaves, finely chopped
60 g prosciutto, finely chopped
$^3/_4$ cup white wine
500 g peeled tomatoes, chopped
1 sprig fresh thyme
2 whole cloves

Put the oxtail, carrot, celery, onion and parsley into a pot with enough water to cover them. Bring to the boil, reduce heat and simmer for 4 hours, skimming frequently. Drain, skim off all fat, discard vegetables and retain stock and meat.

Heat the oil in a pan and add the next 4 ingredients, along with the meat, and sauté until brown. Add the remaining ingredients and stock and simmer for 30 minutes.

Vitello tonnato
Veal in tuna sauce

In this wonderfully tasty and slightly unusual dish the combination of the firm, creamy meat with the stronger flavoured tuna works very well. The capers accent both the veal and fish flavours.

1.5 kg veal nut (fillet cut from the leg)
20 g anchovy fillets
3 cloves garlic, sliced
2 carrots, chopped
2 sticks celery, chopped
2 spring onions, chopped
3 sprigs parsley, chopped
5 cups chicken broth (see page 34) or
   5 cups hot water and 2 teaspoons chicken stock
   powder
$1^1/_2$ cups white wine

Tuna sauce
2 tablespoons capers, chopped
25 g anchovy fillets, drained
1 egg
1 x 185 g tin tuna (in oil, brine or water), drained
juice of 1 lemon
$^1/_2$ cup cream

Make 2 long cuts in the fillet, fill with the anchovy fillets and slices of garlic, and place in a pot. Add the carrots, celery, onion, parsley, chicken broth and wine and bring to a boil. Reduce the heat and simmer, partly covered for $1^1/_2$ to 2 hours. Remove the veal to a plate and keep warm. Strain out the vegetables and save $^1/_4$ cup of this stock to use in the sauce.

Put all the sauce ingredients except the cream into a blender and purée. Pour into a bowl and stir in the cream and the $^1/_4$ cup veal stock.

Cut the veal into slices and arrange on a plate, pour the sauce over them and garnish with chopped parsley.

Stufato di manzo
Beef stew

Marinade
1 red pepper
$1/4$ teaspoon each salt and pepper
pinch ground nutmeg
$1/2$ teaspoon thyme, chopped
1 small bay leaf
$1/2$ teaspoon celery seed
2 cloves garlic, crushed
2 cups white wine

1.5 kg lean beef, chuck steak or similar

2 tablespoons oil
1 onion, chopped
6 rashers bacon, chopped
5 cloves garlic, chopped

Mix all the ingredients for the marinade together. Cut the beef into cubes and add to the marinade. Cover and place in the refrigerator overnight.

Heat the oil in a large frying pan and sauté the onion, bacon and garlic until the bacon is well browned. Pick out the meat from the marinade and add to the onion, bacon and garlic. Fry for 5–10 minutes.

Drain the marinade and add the liquid to the meat. Bring to the boil. Reduce the heat and simmer, covered, for about 2 hours or until the meat is tender. If more liquid is required during the cooking time, add some more wine or beef broth (see page 33).

Manzo alla pizzaiola
Beef pizzaiola

This is wiener schnitzel made in the Italian way. Use 1 schnitzel per person; I have given quantities for 4 people but you can easily increase or decrease as necessary. Serves 4.

4 beef schnitzels
1 tablespoon olive oil
20 g butter
5 cloves garlic, sliced
1 x 400 g tin peeled tomatoes, chopped
1 teaspoon oregano, chopped
2 tablespoons pesto (see page 51) or
  2 tablespoons chopped basil leaves

Melt the oil and butter in a large frying pan and sauté the garlic until tender. Add the tomatoes, oregano and pesto and bring to the boil. Whizz in a food processor or mash up with a potato masher and return to the pan to simmer gently for a further 5 minutes.

Place the meat in the sauce and bring to the boil. Turn the meat once and cook a further 2-4 minutes or until the meat is tender. Serve with a little sauce over each piece.

Falsomagro
Filled meat roll

This classic Sicilian dish is usually made with veal, but I have adapted it slightly for beef schnitzel. There is a long list of ingredients and the method may sound complicated but it's not really difficult and the final product is delicious.

3 tablespoons olive oil
2 cloves garlic, chopped
1 onion, chopped
1 carrot, chopped
1 celery stalk, chopped
1 x 450 g tin tomatoes, peeled and chopped
$\frac{1}{2}$ cup red wine
2–3 large beef schnitzels (about 600 g)
250 g lean mince beef
1 cup dried breadcrumbs
$\frac{1}{2}$ cup parmesan, grated
1 egg
$\frac{1}{4}$ teaspoon salt
$\frac{1}{4}$ teaspoon pepper
4–5 slices cooked ham
150 g provolone or mozzarella, sliced
6–10 cloves garlic, peeled (optional)

Heat the oil in a saucepan large enough to hold the meat roll. Sauté the vegetables until tender. Pour into a food processor and whizz briefly to make a coarse sauce. Pour back into the pan and simmer gently while you assemble the meat.

Lay the schnitzel on a clean, damp teatowel so that it forms a single layer in roughly an oblong shape. Mix the mince, breadcrumbs, parmesan, egg, salt and pepper and spread over the schnitzel almost to the edge. Place a row of ham slices down the middle on top of the mince and place the slices of cheese on top of that. If you are using the garlic, then now is the time to lay a row of peeled garlic cloves along the centre of the cheese layer.

Roll the whole lot up into a long log, using the teatowel. Tie the log with string or dental floss (not minted or fluoridated!), poking the ends neatly into the log as you go.

Place the meat roll on top of the vegetables and pour in the wine and enough water just to cover the meat. Bring to the boil, reduce the heat and simmer gently for 60-90 minutes or until the meat is cooked.

Place the meat roll on a serving platter and keep warm. Make a sauce by boiling the liquid in the pot down until it is reduced by half. Or thicken it by mixing 4 tablespoons flour and enough cold water to make a smooth paste, stir this into the boiling sauce and continue cooking until the sauce thickens.

To serve, remove the string from the meat roll and cut slices about 2 cm thick to place on the serving platter. Pour some of the sauce over the sliced meat and take the rest to the table in a jug.

Ossobuco
Braised shin of veal

You can make this recipe using other types of shins. Veal is expensive and sometimes difficult to get here but that shouldn't put you off making this absolutely delicious and tasty dish. Ossobuco means 'bone with a hole' so get your butcher to saw off the two ends of the shins (the back shanks are best) and to cut the shins into 5 cm pieces so that the meat all cooks evenly.

This is a speciality of Milan so be sure to order it next time you're there and see how your version compares with the real thing. This is one of the few Italian meat dishes that is served with rice (usually the meat course stands alone). Traditionally it is served with Risotto alla milanese (see page 41).

1 quantity tritto (see page 82)
2 shanks of veal cut into 5 cm pieces (see above)
$1/2$ cup flour
1 cup dry white wine
2 cups chicken broth (see page 34) or
  2 cups hot water and 1 chicken stock cube
1 x 400 g tin peeled tomatoes, coarsely chopped
1 teaspoon parsley, chopped
2 teaspoons basil pesto (optional)

Pre-heat the oven to 180°C.

Heat the tritto vegetables in a frying pan until they are tender. Remove the vegetables to a casserole dish leaving the oil in the pan. Dredge the shanks in flour and fry in the oil until brown on all sides. Remove the shanks from the pan and place them on top of the vegetables in the casserole dish.

Pour off any excess oil from the pan, add the wine and boil for a few minutes to loosen any vegetable or meat juices that may be there. Add the chicken broth and tomatoes and simmer together for 5 minutes. Stir in the parsley and basil pesto and pour the lot over the shanks in the casserole dish.

Cover the dish and bake for $1^1/2$–2 hours or until the shanks are tender. Check occasionally that there is sufficient liquid in the casserole so that it doesn't dry out. If more liquid is required, add a little warm water.

Trito

This combination of vegetables preserved in oil is often used when roasting meat and sometimes in fish dishes. Make several times this quantity and store it in separate jars so that you can easily use it in any roast dish to give it an Italian flavour. This recipe makes 1 quantity of trito.

2 carrots, peeled and finely chopped
1 large onion, finely chopped
4 cloves garlic, peeled and chopped
1 stalk celery, finely chopped
1 bay leaf
1 teaspoon fresh rosemary, chopped
olive oil to cover

Tightly pack all the ingredients into a clean jar and add enough olive oil to cover the vegetables. Seal the jars and store in the refrigerator until required. They should keep for months this way.

Porchetta ubriaca
Drunken pork roast

1.5 kg boned pork
2 tablespoons parsley, chopped
3 cloves garlic, chopped
5 juniper berries, crushed
salt and pepper
$^3/_4$ cup grappa

Open out the boned pork and sprinkle the parsley, garlic, juniper berries and salt and pepper on the middle. Fold in half and roll into a cylinder shape. Tie with dental floss (not minted or fluoridated) and place in a plastic bag without holes. Pour in the grappa and leave to marinate in the refrigerator for a couple of hours.

Pre-heat the oven to 180°C. Remove the bag and place the pork in a roasting dish just large enough to hold it. Pour any leftover marinade into a bowl and use it to baste the pork during the roasting time. Sprinkle the pork with salt and pepper and roast for about 2 hours or until the meat is cooked, basting occasionally.

Coniglio con agnello arrosto
Roasted lamb with rabbit

Rabbit is becoming more widely available these days but you can use chicken breast instead. You may also substitute a dry sherry for the Marsala.

3 tablespoons olive oil
2 kg lean lamb, cut in cubes
1 large rabbit, cleaned and jointed
6 cloves garlic, chopped
1 large onion, chopped
3 sprigs fresh rosemary
10 large fresh sage leaves
1$^{1}/_{2}$ cups dry white wine
$^{1}/_{4}$ cup Marsala
salt and pepper

Pre-heat the oven to 180°C. Heat the oil in a casserole dish and brown about a third of the meat at a time so that it is brown on all sides.

Remove the meat and sauté the onions and garlic until tender. Add the rosemary, sage, wine and sherry and simmer gently for a few minutes. Add the browned meats, cover and bake for 1$^{1}/_{2}$ hours or until the meat is tender. Adjust the seasoning and add salt and pepper if necessary.

Costolette d'agnello e parmigiano
Lamb chops and parmesan

Frenched cutlets of lamb are best for this recipe. For a fancier meal I have also made it with noisettes of lamb cut into thin slices. It is wonderful served with fresh pasta gialla or verde (see pages 47–48) cut into tagliatelle.

12–15 lamb chops
$^{1}/_{2}$ cup parmesan cheese, finely grated
2 eggs, beaten
1 cup dried breadcrumbs
salt and pepper
olive oil

Put the parmesan into a plate and press the chops into it to coat both sides. Beat the eggs on a plate and dip the chops into the mixture. Mix the breadcrumbs, salt and pepper on a plate and dip the chops in it to coat both sides. Place in the refrigerator while you heat the oil.

When the oil is hot, fry the chops a few at a time so that they are not crowded in the pan. Remove to drain on some absorbent paper and keep warm while you fry the remaining chops.

Coscia di montone arrosto
Pot-roasted leg of mutton

1 kg leg or shoulder of mutton
4 tablespoons olive oil
5 cloves garlic, chopped
2 sprigs rosemary, chopped
$^1/_2$ cup dry white wine
3 tablespoons dry white wine

Heat the oil in a pot that is just big enough to hold the lamb. Fry the meat so it is brown on all sides then add the garlic and fry until it just begins to brown. Add the rosemary and the $^1/_2$ cup of wine, cover and cook for 90 minutes or until the meat is tender.

Remove the meat from the pot and keep warm. Pour off all but 3 tablespoons of the juices, add the 3 tablespoons of wine and scrape together the pan juices and mash the cooked garlic to form a sauce. Pour over the lamb and serve.

Agnello arrosto
Roasted lamb

This recipe is for a whole lamb but you can make it with smaller quantities by adjusting the cooking times. Serve with boiled new potatoes.

1 x 4 kg lamb
olive oil
salt and pepper
10–12 cloves garlic
8–10 rashers bacon
white wine to baste with

Pre-heat the oven to 170°C.

Rub the lamb with oil and sprinkle with salt and pepper. Make several slits all over the meat and insert the garlic cloves. Place the meat in the roasting pan and lay the strips of bacon over it.

Bake for $2^1/_2$–3 hours or until the meat is tender. Baste with white wine and drippings from the pan occasionally during the baking time.

Arrosto di agnello al ginepro
Lamb and juniper berry roast

Both lamb and mutton are delicious made in this way. The juniper berries, which can be bought from most supermarkets these days, enhance the flavour of the meat and reduce the often fatty taste of sheep meat.

1x 5 kg leg of lamb or mutton
1 quantity tritto (see page 82)
1 cup dry white wine
1 sprig fresh rosemary or
 $^1/_2$ teaspoon dried rosemary
1$^1/_2$ tablespoons juniper berries

Pre-heat the oven to 170°C.

Put all the ingredients into a roasting dish and cover. Roast for 90 minutes. Remove the cover and spoon off any excess oil and continue cooking, uncovered, for 30 minutes. Adjust seasoning with salt and pepper and serve.

Spezzatino d'agnello
Lamb stew

1 quantity tritto (see page 82)
1 kg lean lamb or mutton, cubed
salt and pepper
$^1/_2$ cup dry white wine
5–6 small white onions
$^1/_2$ cup beef broth (see page 33) or
 $^1/_2$ cup hot water and 1 teaspoon beef stock powder

Sauté the tritto in a large pot until the vegetables are tender, about 3 minutes. Add the meat, and cook a further 5 minutes. Add the salt and pepper and wine and bring to a boil, then add the remaining ingredients, cover and cook for 20–25 minutes or until the meat is tender. Serve with fresh fettuccine, rice or new potatoes.

Pollo
Chicken

Pollo ai chiodi di garofano con polenta
Clove chicken and polenta

The polenta here is cooked in a broth, which makes it much tastier than when it is cooked only with water.

1 large chicken
1 onion
10 whole cloves
2 tablespoons oil
50 g butter
2 cups celery, chopped
1 teaspoon sage, chopped
1 cup white wine
$1/4$ cup chicken broth (see page 34) or
   $1/4$ cup hot water and $1/4$ teaspoon chicken stock
   powder
$1/2$ cup tomato purée
fresh sage leaves

Polenta
$3^1/2$ cups coarsely ground cornmeal
2 litres chicken broth (see page 34) or
   2 litres hot water and 2 tablespoons chicken stock
   powder
2 tablespoons butter

Rinse the chicken and salt the cavity. Stud the onion with the cloves and place inside the chicken.

Heat the oil and butter in a pot just slightly bigger than the chicken. Gently sauté the celery until it is tender, then add the sage and stir together. Place the chicken on top of the celery, cover and cook for 10 minutes.

Turn the chicken and add the wine and broth and cook uncovered for 15 minutes. Stir in the tomato purée, cover and cook a further 15–20 minutes.

Remove the chicken to a baking dish and bake at 200°C for 15 minutes or until the chicken is cooked and golden brown. Joint the chicken and discard the clove-studded onion.

While the chicken is cooking make the polenta by bringing the broth to the boil in a large pot and slowly stirring in the cornmeal. Reduce the heat and simmer for about 1 hour, stirring often so that the polenta cooks evenly and without lumps. It should be so thick that your spoon almost stands up in it.

Spoon the polenta into a serving platter and place the jointed chicken on top with sauce spooned over each piece. Garnish with fresh sage leaves.

Pollo al limone
Lemon-roasted chicken

This is the simplest and most delicious way I know of cooking a chicken. You really must try it!

1 chicken split open at the breast
3 juicy lemons
salt
olive oil
1 teaspoon oregano, fresh or dried
5 cloves garlic

Lay the chicken out, skin side up, in a roasting pan. Squeeze the lemons over the chicken, sprinkle with salt and oregano and rub with the oil. Poke the garlic in under the wings, under the breast and wherever else you can. Allow to marinate for at least 1 hour.

Pour 2 cups of water around the bird (not over it) and roast at 180°C for $1^1/_4$ hours. Remove the chicken from the roasting dish and keep it warm while you make a gravy with the remnants in the pan.

Pollo alla Mamma Rosa
Mamma Rosa chicken

This recipe for Italian-style chicken cooked on a bed of onion and blanketed with wine and tomatoes comes from an Italian emigrée friend.

2 large onions, chopped
5 cloves garlic, chopped
1.5 kg chicken, jointed (or chicken pieces)
$^2/_3$ cup white wine
1 x 400 g tin peeled tomatoes, chopped
2 tablespoons parsley, chopped

Put the onions and garlic in a large frying pan and place the jointed chicken on top of them. Cook for 10 minutes, turning the chicken once.

When the onions begin to brown pour over the wine and cook a further 2 minutes, then add the tomatoes and parsley.

Cover and cook a further 15–20 minutes, turning once or twice as required until the chicken is cooked.

Pollo alla marengo
Chicken Marengo style

This delicious, delicately flavoured combination of chicken, mushrooms and herbs takes its name from the Marengo area of Piedmont.

1.5 kg chicken, jointed (or chicken pieces)
salt and pepper
$^1/_4$ teaspoon ground nutmeg
$^1/_3$ cup flour
2 tablespoons olive oil
50 g butter
1 teaspoon fresh rosemary, chopped
3 sage leaves, chopped
2 tablespoons parsley, chopped
$^1/_4$ cup white wine
$^1/_4$ cup brandy
1 tablespoon flour
1 cup hot chicken broth (see page 34) or
    1 cup hot water and 1 chicken stock cube
300 g button mushrooms, sliced
2 lemons

Dredge the chicken in the flour, salt and pepper and nutmeg. Melt the oil and butter in a large frying pan and fry the chicken, turning to brown on all sides.

Remove the chicken and add the rosemary, sage, parsley, wine and brandy, bring to the boil and then add the chicken broth. Mix the flour with a little water and stir into the sauce.

Replace the chicken in the sauce, cover and simmer gently for 15 minutes. Add the mushrooms and continue cooking for 5 minutes. Squeeze the juice from the lemon over the chicken in the sauce, garnish with parsley and serve with plain pasta or rice.

Pollo alla romana
Chicken Roman style

$^1/_4$ cup olive oil
1 small onion, chopped
3 cloves garlic, chopped
1.5 kg chicken, jointed (or chicken pieces)
1 x 400 g tin peeled tomatoes, chopped
1 large green capsicum, cut in strips
salt and pepper

Heat the oil in a large frying pan and sauté the onion and garlic. Add the chicken pieces and brown all over. Add the tomatoes and capsicum, cover and gently simmer for 30 minutes or until the chicken is cooked. Adjust seasoning with salt and pepper if necessary and serve with plain rice.

Pollo arrosto
Pot-roasted chicken

Originally, chicken was roasted in a pot because ovens weren't reliable. Today, of course, that's no longer a problem but this is still a tasty way of cooking poultry.

2 tablespoons olive oil
50 g butter
1.5 kg chicken, jointed (or chicken pieces)
5 cloves garlic, chopped
1 teaspoon fresh rosemary, chopped
$^1/_2$ cup white wine
salt and pepper
3 tablespoons white wine

Melt the butter and oil in a heavy-bottomed pot and brown the chicken on all sides. Add the garlic, rosemary and seasoning and cook for 2 minutes. Pour in the $^1/_2$ cup of wine, cover and cook over a low heat for 20–25 minutes or until the chicken is done, turning occasionally.

Remove the chicken and drain off all but 3 tablespoons of the remaining oil. Add the 3 tablespoons wine and scrape together the cooking juices and mash the cooked garlic to form a sauce. Pour this over the chicken and serve.

Pollo arrosto con rosmarino
Oven-roasted chicken and rosemary

1.5 kg chicken
salt and pepper
2 sprigs rosemary
8 cloves garlic
1 quantity tritto (see page 82)
$^1/_2$ cup white wine

Pre-heat the oven to 180°C and lightly oil a casserole dish which is just big enough to hold the chicken. Sprinkle salt and pepper on both the inside and outside of the chicken and put the garlic cloves into the chicken's cavity.

Place the sprigs of rosemary on the bottom of the dish and place the chicken on top. Spoon the tritto over the bird and bake for 1 hour or until cooked. Baste the chicken a few times while it is cooking.

Remove the chicken and keep warm. Pour off any excess oil and discard the rosemary. Put the dish on an element and add the wine. Scrape together the juices and vegetables and simmer for 2 minutes. Pour this over the chicken and serve.

Pollo e porcini
Chicken and mushrooms

Porcini mushrooms are very flavourful and really make this dish special. If you can't get porcini, however, you can use 500 g of sliced fresh mushrooms instead – these, of course, don't need to be soaked.

15 g dried porcini mushrooms
1 cup hot water
2 tablespoons olive oil
25 g butter
1.5 kg chicken, jointed (or chicken pieces)
$^1/_4$ cup tomato purée
salt and pepper

Soak the porcini in the hot water for 10 minutes. When they are soft, chop them coarsely and return to the water.

Heat the oil and butter in a heavy-bottomed pan and fry the chicken so that it is brown on all sides.

Pour over the chicken the mushrooms and the water in which they were soaking and stir in the tomato purée. Season with salt and pepper, cover and simmer over a low heat for 20–25 minutes or until the chicken is cooked.

Pollo alla cacciatora
Chicken cacciatore

This is like chicken chasseur but with an Italian touch. If possible, serve with it the same type of red wine you used to cook the chicken.

3 tablespoons olive oil
30 g butter
1.5 kg chicken, jointed
1 teaspoon fresh rosemary, chopped
3 cloves garlic, sliced
5 anchovy fillets, well drained and chopped
$^1/_2$ cup cider vinegar
1 cup red wine
3 tablespoons tomato paste
$^1/_2$ cup chicken broth (see page 34) or
    $^1/_2$ cup hot water and $^1/_2$ teaspoon chicken stock
    powder

Heat the oil and butter in a large frying pan and brown the chicken on all sides. Mix the rosemary, garlic, anchovies, vinegar and red wine together and pour over the chicken. Simmer gently for 10 minutes.

Mix the tomato paste and the chicken broth together and add this to the chicken. Simmer uncovered for a further 15–20 minutes or until the chicken is cooked.

Le verdure e le insalate
Vegetables and salads

Most people think of Italian cuisine and tomatoes as having been together forever. In truth, it was only with the return of sailors from the New World (a mere 500 years ago) that tomatoes, potatoes and even red peppers became a part of Italian cooking culture. But once such vegetables were introduced, the Italians took to them wholeheartedly and created some of the most delicious dishes possible.

Even though one can now buy very good quality frozen or tinned vegetables, there is nothing quite like the taste of fresh vegetables in season. Italian cooking tries to ensure that the vegetables taste like themselves and that their beautiful colours are preserved as much as possible.

Carciofi dorati
Golden artichokes

Deep-fried globe artichokes cooked in this way can be served as a vegetable dish or as part of an antipasti platter (with the chilli mayonnaise in the Bocconcini fritti recipe on page 16). They are delicious served as they are or with a sauce. You can buy marinated artichoke hearts from the deli or use fresh small artichokes and clean them as outlined below.

**12–15 baby artichokes or marinated artichoke hearts
1 lemon
batter (see Melanzane alla parmigiana, page 96)
olive oil**

Cut the base and remove the hard outer leaves of the artichokes. If the choke is quite tough and spiky you will need to remove that too, simply by cutting it out with a sharp knife. You will be left with the heart or perhaps the heart and some of the softer leaves around it. After each artichoke has been prepared in this way drop it into a bowl of cold water with the juice from the lemon added.

If you're using marinated artichoke hearts none of the above is necessary.

Make the batter according to the recipe on page 96. Heat the oil. Remove the artichokes from the water and pat them dry. Slice them into quarters and dip them in the batter. Fry in the oil until they are golden. Drain on absorbent paper and serve hot.

Carciofi fritti
Crisp-fried artichokes

Whole small artichokes deep-fried so that the leaves are crisp and the hearts are tender.

12–15 small artichokes, with stalks on
1 lemon
olive oil
salt and pepper

Remove all the tough outer leaves of the artichokes and peel the outside of the stalk. If the choke is spiky you will have to cut it out with a sharp knife. As you prepare each artichoke, place it in a large bowl with cold water and the juice from the lemon.

Remove from the water and pat dry, being sure to remove as much water as possible. Sprinkle with salt.

Heat a little oil in a frying pan and fry a few artichokes at a time over a gentle heat for 8–10 minutes. This is to more or less cook the inside of the artichoke. Drain on absorbent paper while you cook the remaining artichokes in the same way. Leave the cooked artichokes for about 1 hour before proceeding to the next stage.

Heat more oil in the frying pan so that it is about 5 cm deep. Hold each artichoke by the stalk and dip it upside down into the hot oil for a few seconds. The leaves should open out and fry crisply. Drain on absorbent paper.

Asparagi alla milanese
Asparagus with parmesan

To really appreciate its taste, it is best to cook and present such a beautiful and delicious vegetable as asparagus in the simplest of ways. This recipe from northern Italy does just that. Serve on oval dish to show off the spears to best advantage.

2 kg fresh asparagus spears
$\frac{1}{2}$ cup fresh parmesan, grated
100 g butter
ground black pepper

Wash the asparagus, snap off any hard parts near the cut ends and place the spears in a large saucepan or frying pan with a lid. Add enough water just to cover the asparagus, cover and bring to the boil.

Cook for 5–10 minutes so that the spears are still green and just beginning to droop at their tips. Drain and place on the warmed serving platter.

Sprinkle with the grated parmesan. Melt the butter and pour over the asparagus.

Pomodori gratinati
Baked tomatoes (1)

Tomatoes baked in this tasty, simple and colourful way are ideal for a buffet table. They also make a good side dish to a main meal or lunch.

6 large ripe tomatoes, cut in half
salt and pepper
$^1/_4$ cup extra virgin olive oil
4 tablespoons fresh oregano, chopped
4 tablespoons parsley, chopped
$^1/_4$ cup dried breadcrumbs

Lightly oil a shallow casserole dish and place the tomatoes cut side up in it. Season with a little salt and pepper. Mix the oil, oregano, parsley and breadcrumbs together and spoon over the tomatoes. Bake at 180°C for 35–40 minutes. Serve hot.

Pomodori gratinati
Baked tomatoes (2)

Keep this recipe for when you have lots of time. The long, slow cooking concentrates the sweet tomato flavour. Serve hot on crostini as an appetiser or as a side dish to a main meal.

12 ripe tomatoes
4 cloves garlic, sliced
salt

Pre-heat the oven to 120°C.
    Cut the tomatoes in half and place in a baking dish cut side up. Sprinkle each half with a little salt and place a slice or two of garlic on each. Bake for 4–5 hours. Serve hot.

Frittata di cavolfiore
Cauliflower frittata

This cauliflower omelette makes a very tasty light meal or side dish.

2 cups cauliflower florets
1/4 cup olive oil
6–8 anchovy fillets, chopped
6 eggs
2 tablespoons capers, chopped and drained
chopped parsley

Cut cauliflower into small florets and boil in salted water for 10 minutes. Drain. In a frying pan heat oil and sauté the cauliflower and anchovies for a few minutes.

Beat the eggs, add the capers and pour over the cauliflower mixture. Cover and cook until golden on the bottom.

Once it is cooked, remove the lid and place the pan under the grill for a few minutes more so that it is golden on top. Then simply slide the frittata out of the pan and onto the serving platter. Garnish with chopped parsley and serve at once.

Carote e funghi
Carrots and mushrooms

Although so simple that it is almost embarrassing, this combination of vegetables is not often done here in New Zealand.

4–5 carrots, peeled and cut in matchsticks
250 g button mushrooms, cleaned and sliced
50 g butter
1/4 cup parsley, chopped
1 lemon

Bring a pot of salted water to the boil and add the carrots. Bring the water back to the boil and cook the carrots until they are just tender, about 2 minutes, then drain.

Melt the butter in a frying pan and sauté the mushrooms for a few minutes. Add the carrots and parsley and squeeze the lemon into the pan. Stir together and cook until all the ingredients are warm. Serve warm.

Melanzane alla parmigiana
Eggplant with parmesan

This dish consists of layers of deep-fried, battered eggplant, tomato sauce and parmesan. The batter used here is ideal for other fish and vegetable dishes that require a batter.

3 tablespoons extra virgin olive oil
3 cloves garlic, chopped
600 g ripe tomatoes, peeled and chopped
5–10 leaves fresh basil, chopped
1 cup parmesan, grated
1–2 eggplants (about 500 g), peeled

Batter
2 eggs, separated
1 cup flour
$^2/_3$ cup white wine or
  $^2/_3$ cup water
1 tablespoon extra virgin olive oil
pinch ground nutmeg

Make the batter by mixing the egg yolks, flour, wine or water, oil and nutmeg together and leaving for 30 minutes. Then, just before you intend using the batter, beat the egg whites to stiff peaks and fold them into the flour mixture.

Heat the oil in a pan and sauté the garlic briefly, then add the tomatoes and basil and bring to the boil. Pour into a food processor and whizz briefly, then return to the pan and simmer gently for about 25–30 minutes to reduce.

Heat some extra oil to deep-fry the eggplant. Slice the eggplants into 1–2 cm thick slices and dip in the batter. Fry, turning once to brown on both sides. Drain on absorbent paper.

Spoon about a third of the sauce into the bottom of a casserole dish and place a layer of the fried eggplant on it. Cover with sauce and sprinkle with a third of the parmesan. Layer the remaining eggplant, cover with the rest of the sauce and then sprinkle the remaining two-thirds of the parmesan on top. Bake at 180°C for 25–30 minutes. Allow to cool for a few minutes before serving.

Cavolfiore all'acciughe
Cauliflower with anchovy

1 cauliflower (about 1.5 kg)
$^1/_2$ cup extra virgin olive oil
3 cloves garlic, chopped
3 tablespoons breadcrumbs
6 anchovy fillets, mashed

Trim the cauliflower, cook in boiling salted water until barely tender, drain and keep warm.

Heat the oil, add the garlic, breadcrumbs and anchovies and cook for 2 minutes, stirring constantly. Pour this sauce over the cauliflower and serve.

Fagiolini al pomodoro
Green beans in tomato sauce

1 kg fresh green beans, sliced in 3–4 cm pieces
$^1/_4$ cup extra virgin olive oil
3 cloves garlic, chopped
500 g ripe tomatoes, peeled and chopped
$^1/_2$ cup hot vegetable broth (see page 32) or
   $^1/_2$ cup hot water and $^1/_2$ teaspoon vegetable stock
   powder

Heat the oil in a pan and sauté the garlic until it begins to brown, then add the beans and cook for a few minutes. Add the tomatoes and vegetable stock and bring to a boil.

Reduce the heat, cover and simmer for 25–30 minutes or until the beans are cooked. Stir occasionally to ensure even cooking.

Fagiolini brasati
Braised green beans

1 kg fresh green beans
$^1/_3$ cup olive oil
3 cloves garlic, crushed
2 tablespoons parsley, chopped
salt and pepper

If your beans are quite young you don't need to top and tail them as you do older beans. Wash the beans and slice them in half on the diagonal. Drop into a pot of boiling water and cook for 5 minutes. Drain.

Heat the oil, garlic and half of the parsley in an ovenproof dish. Add the beans, tossing to coat with the oil mixture, cover and cook at 150°C for a further 10 minutes or until the beans are tender. Serve on a warmed plate garnished with the remaining parsley and a sprinkle of salt and pepper.

Patate alla panna
Potatoes and cream

This is a bit like potatoes au gratin made in a frying pan.

3 tablespoons extra virgin olive oil
1 onion, chopped
3 rashers bacon, chopped
1 kg potatoes, peeled and thinly sliced
2 cups chicken broth (see page 34) or
   2 cups hot water and 2 chicken stock cubes
$1/_2$ cup cream
pepper

Heat the oil and sauté the onion and bacon. Add the sliced potatoes and hot broth and bring to the boil. Reduce the heat, cover and simmer gently for 20-25 minutes or until the potatoes are cooked.

A few minutes before serving pour in the cream and warm through. Grind a little pepper over and serve.

Patate al limone
Potatoes with lemon

Simple mashed potatoes with a dash of lemon, this sounds an unusual combination but the taste is lovely.

8–10 potatoes (about 1.5 kg)
2 tablespoons butter
freshly ground pepper
milk
grated rind of 1 large lemon

Peel and quarter the potatoes and boil until just cooked. Drain well and place in a food mixer with the butter, grated lemon rind and freshly ground pepper to taste. Blend to purée the potato while adding enough milk to make a smooth but firm mixture. Serve while warm.

Patate alle olive
Potatoes with olives and anchovies

1 kg potatoes, cut into wedges
$^1/_4$ cup olive oil
$^2/_3$ cup black olives, pitted
6 anchovy fillets, chopped
1 tablespoon parsley, chopped

Heat the oil in a pan and add the potato wedges. Sprinkle with the chopped anchovies, cover and cook for 30 minutes, turning occasionally. Just before serving add the olives and heat through. Turn into a serving dish and sprinkle with parsley.

Zucchine alla cipolle
Zucchini with onion sauce

6 small zucchini
4 tablespoons olive oil
1 onion, finely chopped
1 clove garlic, chopped
$^1/_2$ capsicum, chopped
$^1/_4$ teaspoon oregano, dried or fresh

Slice the zucchini in half lengthwise and boil until just tender. Heat the oil in a pan and sauté the other vegetables until soft, then purée to make the sauce. Drain the zucchini and put on the serving plate. Cover with the sauce and serve.

Parmigiana di zucchine
Zucchini with parmesan and tomatoes

So delicious that you could serve it with potatoes as a vegetarian meal, this dish originates in Tuscany but could just as easily have come from anywhere in Italy. It makes use of garden-fresh zucchini, basil and tomatoes as well mozzarella and parmesan.

3–4 average-sized zucchini
$^1/_2$ cup olive oil
6 cloves garlic, chopped
500 g tomatoes, peeled and chopped
1 cup fresh basil leaves
400 g mozzarella, sliced
200 g parmesan, grated

Slice the zucchini about 10–15 mm thick and fry them on both sides in the oil. Drain on absorbent paper and set aside.

Pour off all but about 3 tablespoons of the oil and fry the garlic for about 1 minute. Add the tomatoes and $^1/_4$ cup of the basil and simmer for about 15 minutes until the sauce thickens slightly. Season with salt and pepper to taste.

Spoon about a third of the sauce on the bottom of a baking dish and lay the fried zucchini on top of it. Lay the mozzarella slices on that, then the basil leaves and then the remaining sauce. Spread the grated parmesan over the top and bake at 180°C for 25–30 minutes.

Le insalate
Salads

In Italy a salad with lettuce in it generally contains only one kind of lettuce, so that the flavour can stand alone and not be complicated by other tastes. Particularly good lettuces are curly endive, cos, chicory, lamb's ear and radicchio. Seeds and seedlings can be bought at garden centres and the lettuces are best when grown and picked fresh from your garden. Some greens are particularly strong or bitter and they are picked for just those qualities. For example, a salad might consist of endive leaves only.

Herbs are also best fresh from the garden. A typical selection of salad herbs would be basil, sorrel, chives, oregano and mint.

Salads are dressed very simply with about 1 teaspoon sea salt and a dash of fresh ground pepper, 1 tablespoon vinegar and a splash of extra virgin olive oil (about $1/4$ cup). Mix the whole lot well in a jar and pour over the salad. It is important to toss the salad well to coat all the greens.

Insalata verde
Simple Italian salad

This typically simple green salad is dressed with a very simple oil and vinegar dressing.

4–5 cups cos lettuce, cleaned
1 clove garlic, crushed
$1^1/_2$ tablespoons red wine vinegar
pinch salt
$1/_3$ cup extra virgin olive oil

Drain the lettuce well and tear leaves into a large serving bowl. Mix the garlic, wine vinegar, salt and oil together in a jar and pour over the salad just before serving. Toss lightly and serve.

Insalata di pomodori
Tomato salad

A simple tomato salad with an oil and vinegar dressing.

4–6 ripe tomatoes
1 tablespoon fresh basil, chopped
3 tablespoons cider vinegar
$1/4$ teaspoon salt
$1/3$ cup extra virgin olive oil

Cut the tomatoes into 1 cm thick slices and arrange on a serving plate. Mix the dressing ingredients in a jar and spoon over the tomatoes before serving.

Fagiolini all'agro
Fresh green bean salad

1 kg fresh green beans
1 tablespoon cider vinegar
1 clove garlic, crushed
pinch chopped red pepper
$1/3$ cup extra virgin olive oil

Cut the beans diagonally into 3 cm long pieces. Bring a pot of salted water to the boil and add the beans. Bring the water back to the boil and time for 10 minutes. Drain in a colander and rinse under cold water.

Mix the dressing ingredients together in a jar. Put the beans in the serving bowl and pour the dressing over them. Cover and refrigerate for 1 hour before serving.

Insalata mista all'Italiana
Combination Italian-style salad

It's the balsamic vinegar dressing that makes this salad so Italian and so delicious. In this case the combination of different lettuces gives a greater depth of character and a wider variety of tastes.

5 cups of a variety of lettuce leaves
(e.g. iceberg, rocket cress, endive, chicory or radicchio)

Dressing
3 tablespoons balsamic vinegar
$^1/_2$ teaspoon salt
2 cloves garlic, crushed
$^1/_2$ teaspoon dried mustard
pinch ground pepper
6 tablespoons extra virgin olive oil

Wash the lettuce leaves well and discard any hard or wilted parts. Tear into pieces and place in a large salad bowl.

Make the dressing by putting all the ingredients except the oil into a jar and shaking to mix. Then add the oil and shake again.

Just before serving, pour over the lettuce and toss lightly together.

This dressing keeps for several days and should be made at least 6 hours before it is needed so that the flavours can mingle together.

Pane e pizze
Pizza and bread

Being able to make a good pizza from scratch is a wonderful thing. Because the basic dough is so simple to make and the recipe so easy to remember you'll be able to whip up a pizza almost anywhere. Although there are a number of classic pizza toppings, what you use is really up to you: experiment and find the taste combinations that most appeal to you, your family and friends.

In this section I give you the basic yeast dough recipe and a wholemeal variation. By using either of these you will be able to create your own, personalised pizza.

There are also a couple of sauces which you'll find useful, but you can always use tomato purée or even chopped tomatoes at a pinch.

Further on I have provided several more traditional pizza recipes but even these are simply the yeast base and a specific combination of toppings.

Although pizzas are now considered a fast food, they are also a complete meal. Pizza making and eating should be fun and a tasty experience for all.

Pizza originates in the Campania region where the classic Neapolitan pizza is the standard and others have developed from it. You should eat pizza the same day it is made.

I have also included here 2 bread recipes.

Pizza bases

Here are the only 2 bases you'll need to make any type of pizza your heart desires. These recipes each make sufficient dough for a 30 cm pizza that serves 4–6 people. Use a non-stick pizza pan for best results. You can also cook a pizza on a very lightly oiled baking tray.

Simple yeast dough

1 tablespoon dry yeast
$^1/_2$ teaspoon sugar
1 cup warm water
3 cups flour
4 teaspoons olive oil

Put the yeast, sugar and water in a small bowl and set aside to foam up, which takes about 5 minutes.

In a larger bowl combine the flour and oil, add the yeast mixture and mix well. Turn out onto the counter and knead to a smooth ball.

Put the ball back into the bowl, cover with a teatowel and leave to rise for about 20–30 minutes.

Wholemeal yeast dough

1½ tablespoons dry yeast
½ teaspoon sugar
½ cup warm water
2 cups wholemeal flour
½ teaspoon salt
1 teaspoon oil

Put the yeast, sugar and water in a small bowl and set aside to foam up, which takes about 5 minutes.

In a larger bowl combine the flour and oil, add the yeast mixture and mix well. Turn out onto the counter and knead to a smooth ball.

Put the ball back into the bowl, cover with a teatowel and leave to rise for about 20–30 minutes.

Sauces for pizzas

The sauce for a pizza should be tasty and concentrated, never runny or watery. When spreading the sauce on the pizza be sure to leave about 2–3 cm around the edge. This gives the topping space to spread without overflowing the dough, and leaves a place for holding the pizza when you're eating it. If you're really pushed for time simply use tomato purée and sprinkle with a little dried oregano, or even just chopped tomatoes.

Basic tomato sauce

This simple tomato sauce can be used for pizza, gnocchi or pasta.

1 onion, chopped
3 cloves garlic, chopped
2 teaspoons olive oil
6 tomatoes, peeled
1 teaspoon sugar
1 teaspoon oregano, fresh or dried
½ teaspoon basil, fresh or dried
salt and pepper to taste

Sauté the onion and garlic in the oil until transparent. Add the tomatoes, sugar and herbs and simmer for about 5 minutes until the sauce thickens slightly. Blend until smooth.

Homemade tomato sauce

This will keep for several weeks in the refrigerator or for months in the freezer. I like to freeze it in ice-cube trays and then just defrost a couple of cubes when I need it.

4 teaspoons olive oil
1 large onion, chopped
3 celery stalks, chopped
1 carrot, peeled and chopped
2 cloves garlic, chopped
6–8 large tomatoes, chopped
1 bay leaf
1 teaspoon sugar
1 teaspoon basil, fresh or dried
1 teaspoon oregano, fresh or dried
2 teaspoons yeasted herb salt or vegetable salt
1 tablespoon chopped parsley
$1/2$ cup vegetable stock

Heat the oil and sauté the onion, celery, carrot and garlic for 5 minutes. Add the tomatoes and cook a further 5 minutes.

Add the seasonings and vegetable stock and simmer for about 30 minutes, stirring occasionally to make sure it doesn't stick.

Remove the bay leaf, purée the sauce in a blender and return to the pan to simmer a few minutes more.

Pizzas

Pizza alla napoletana
Classic Neapolitan pizza

The classic Neapolitan pizza, the mother of all pizzas, is still a popular choice and is so simple.

1 quantity simple yeast dough (see page 104)
4 tablespoons basic tomato sauce (see page 105)
3 large tomatoes, sliced
250 g mozzarella, grated
$1^1/_2$ teaspoons dried oregano
10 anchovy fillets

Pre-heat the oven to 230°C.

Pull and push the dough into a 30 cm pizza pan. Spread the sauce over the base and place the tomato slices over the sauce. Sprinkle with the mozzarella and oregano and criss-cross the anchovy fillets over the top. Bake for about 15 minutes.

Pizza al formaggio
Cheese pizza

For this simple pizza you can use any firm cheese such as cheddar, gouda, gruyere, colby, etc. I use straight parmesan because it is tasty, but if you find this too expensive try using equal amounts of tasty cheddar and parmesan.

1 quantity simple yeast dough (see page 104)
2 eggs
250 g cheese, grated

Pre-heat the oven to 230°C.

Pull and push the dough into the 30 cm pizza pan. Beat the eggs and stir in the grated cheese. Spread the cheese mixture over the base and bake for about 15 minutes.

Pizza ai funghi
Mushroom pizza

With the array of different mushrooms available these days you should be able to make some really interesting mushroom pizzas. Substitute any other cheese if the provolone is unavailable.

1 quantity simple yeast dough (see page 104)
4 tablespoons tomato sauce (see page 105)
450 g fresh mushrooms, sliced
80 g provolone, grated

Pre-heat the oven to 230°C.

Pull and push the dough into the 30 cm pizza pan and spread with the tomato sauce. Place the mushrooms over the sauce and sprinkle with the grated cheese. Bake for about 15 minutes.

Pizza alle acciughe
Anchovy pizza

The strong flavour of the anchovy is mellowed by the mozzarella and complemented nicely by the basil.

1 quantity simple yeast dough (see page 104)
4 tablespoons tomato sauce (see page 105)
45 g tin anchovy fillets, well drained
5 fresh basil leaves, chopped
200 g mozzarella, grated

Pre-heat the oven to 230°C.

Pull and push the dough into the 30 cm pizza pan and spread with the tomato sauce. Sprinkle half of the cheese over the base and criss-cross the anchovies over this. Scatter the basil over the anchovies and sprinkle with the remaining cheese. Bake for about 15 minutes.

Pizza con cavolfiore e speck
Cauliflower and bacon pizza

This may sound unlikely but it is a lovely way to deal with the problem of children not eating their vegetables – although adults, too, will enjoy this pizza.

1 quantity simple yeast dough (see page 104)
4 tablespoons tomato sauce (see page 105)
2 cups cauliflower, broken into florets
1 tablespoon butter
1 teaspoon dry white wine
3 rashers bacon, chopped

Bring a pot of salted water to the boil and add the cauliflower florets. Bring the water back to the boil and then remove from the heat and drain. Add the butter and wine to the cauliflower and mash together coarsely with a potato masher.

Pre-heat the oven to 230°C.

Pull and push the dough into a 30 cm pizza pan and spread with the tomato sauce. Spread the coarsely mashed cauliflower over the sauce and scatter with the chopped bacon. Sprinkle with salt and pepper and drizzle with a little oil. Bake for about 15 minutes.

Pizza all'aglio e pomodoro
Garlic and tomato pizza

A very simple combination of garlic and tomatoes baked together on top of fresh bread.

1 quantity simple yeast dough (see page 104)
2 tablespoons basic tomato sauce (see page 105)
2 tomatoes, peeled and chopped
6 cloves garlic, sliced
3 tablespoons olive oil
salt and pepper

Pre-heat the oven to 230°C.

Pull and push the dough into a 30 cm pizza pan. Spread with the tomato sauce and sprinkle with the chopped tomatoes and sliced garlic. Drizzle with the oil and season with the salt and pepper. Bake for about 15 minutes.

Pizza ai frutti di mare
Seafood pizza

You can add cheese to this pizza if you like. Just sprinkle 1 cup of grated cheese over everything and bake.

1 quantity simple yeast dough (see page 104)
4 tablespoons tomato sauce (see page 105)
$1/4$ cup shrimps, shelled
8 small mussels, shelled
$1/4$ cup cooked squid rings or pieces
8 small cockles, shelled
8 baby octopus

Pre-heat the oven to 230°C.

Pull and push the dough into a 30 cm pizza pan and spread with the tomato sauce. Place the shrimps, mussels, squid and cockles on top of the pizza and bake for about 15 minutes.

Add the octopus to the pizza after it has been cooking for 10 minutes and then finish baking.

Pizza all'agnello
Lamb pizza

Or should this be called the New Zealand pizza? Lamb is very tasty and goes well with the ricotta. You can substitute cottage cheese for ricotta in this recipe.

1 quantity simple yeast dough (see page 104)
4 tablespoons tomato sauce (see page 105)
400 g lean lamb mince
5 cloves garlic, sliced
1 tablespoon parsley, chopped
200 g ricotta cheese
salt and pepper

Pre-heat the oven to 230°C.

Pull and push the dough into a 30 cm pizza pan and spread with the tomato sauce.

Fry the lamb until it is just beginning to turn brown. Drain on absorbent paper and cool. Sprinkle the lamb, garlic and parsley over the sauce and then scatter the ricotta over. Sprinkle with salt and pepper and bake for about 15 minutes.

Calzone
Pocket pizzas

Calzone, sometimes called pocket pizzas, are like a pizza sandwich. They are very convenient for picnics since the filling doesn't slide off or stick to things in transit. You can fill your calzone with the same things you would put on top of your pizza, but use less.

1 quantity yeast dough (see page 104)
$^1/_2$ cup simple tomato sauce (see page 105)
1 cup parmesan, grated
2 tablespoons onion, finely chopped
400 g pepperoni, thinly sliced
8 leaves fresh basil, chopped
3 tablespoons olive oil

Pre-heat the oven to 230° C.

Divide the dough into 8 pieces and roll out into 10 cm diameter circles. Spread half of each circle with some sauce and sprinkle cheese, onion, pepperoni and basil, evenly divided among the 8 pieces.

Fold over the base and seal the edges. Place on a baking sheet and brush with the oil. Bake for about 15 minutes.

Calzone con pomodorini
Tomato calzone

In this simple and tasty combination the mozzarella melts beautifully and its fairly bland flavour does not overpower the tomato. You can also make a wonderfully tasty calzone by using other cheeses to suit your taste.

1 quantity simple yeast dough (see page 104)
400 g fresh tomatoes, chopped
1 cup mozzarella, grated
salt and pepper
oil

Lightly oil a pizza pan and pre-heat the oven to 230°C.

Divide the dough into 8 pieces and roll out into 10 cm diameter circles. Divide the tomato and cheese evenly between the circles and sprinkle with salt and pepper. Fold over the base and seal the edges. Place on a baking sheet and brush with the oil. Bake for about 15 minutes.

Pane
Bread

Schiacciata al rosmarino
Flat bread with rosemary

Serve this as you would freshly baked bread or bread rolls: to accompany soups, main meals, lunches and antipasti.

1 tablespoon dry yeast
$\frac{1}{2}$ teaspoon sugar
1 cup warm water
3 cups flour
3 tablespoons extra virgin olive oil
1 tablespoon rosemary, fresh or dried, chopped
salt

Put the yeast, sugar and warm water into a plastic bowl and let foam. This takes about 10 minutes. Put the flour and oil into a larger plastic bowl, add the yeast mixture and mix well. Turn out onto the counter and knead to a smooth consistency. Form into a ball and replace in the large bowl. Cover with a teatowel and let double in size (about 30 minutes).

Knead and press out onto a baking sheet, cover and let rise about 30 minutes. Brush with oil, sprinkle with salt and rosemary and bake at 230° C for 15 minutes.

Grissini
Bread sticks

Grissini are long, crisp bread sticks that have become synonymous with Italian eating throughout the world. Just about every meal served in the Piedmont area of Italy is accompanied by grissini. You can add finely chopped herbs to the dough to make different flavours, or brush the grissini with beaten egg and sprinkle them with coarse salt, caraway, sesame or dill seeds. Make these bread sticks ahead of time and store them in an airtight container.

1 tablespoon dry yeast
$1/_2$ teaspoon sugar
1 cup warm water
3 cups flour
3 tablespoons extra virgin olive oil
$1/_2$ teaspoon salt

Put the yeast and sugar into a small plastic bowl (plastic is warmer than stainless steel or china) and add the warm water. Leave for about 5 minutes until it foams.

Put the flour, oil and salt into a larger plastic bowl and add the yeast mixture. Mix well, turning out onto the benchtop and kneading to a smooth dough. Shape into a ball, replace in the large bowl, cover and leave to rise for about 30 minutes.

Punch the dough down and knead briefly. Break off pieces about the size of a small lemon and roll into a 2 cm thick sausage shape. Place on a baking tray and brush with oil or beaten egg for a shinier glaze.

Bake at 230°C for 15–20 minutes or until golden brown. Cool completely before storing in an airtight container until required.

I dolci
Desserts

As a rule, Italians save elaborate desserts for special or festive occasions After dinner they more usually finish off with some fresh fruit and perhaps a little cheese. When they do have desserts, however, they really do them well.

This section offers a selection from simple and light to rich and creamy — from granitas and ice creams through biscotti and panforte to the more elaborate desserts such as tiramisu, la zuppa inglese and sambucca cheesecake.

A great dessert must be beautifully presented, exciting to the eye as well as the taste, slightly sinful and always satisfying. Good quality ingredients are very important, and in this area we are well supplied here in New Zealand, with cream, butter, cheeses and superb fruits that are second to none.

I have not given serving amounts for desserts — it all depends on the appetites around the table.

Granitas

Halfway between sherbet and solid water ices, somewhat granular in texture, these little flecks of flavoured ice, delicious and dissolving, provide a sharp chill. Try making any fruit purée — raspberry, strawberry, rock melon, passionfruit — and mixing it according to the following recipe for lemon granita.

Granita di limone
Lemon granita

1/2 cup lemon juice
1/2 cup sugar
2 cups water

Dissolve the sugar in the water and boil for a few minutes to thicken the syrup slightly. Remove from the heat and stir in the lemon juice.

Pour into a shallow metal tray and freeze, stirring occasionally. Just before serving transfer to a blender and whizz to a slush. Or simply scrape with a fork to get mounds of granular frozen granita.

Granita di arancia
Orange granita

2 oranges, sliced
125 g sugar
2 cups water
1²/₃ cups orange juice

Put the slices of orange into a pot with the sugar and water. Bring to a boil and simmer for a few minutes. Remove the orange slices and stir in the orange juice.

Put this mixture into a shallow tray (steel if you have it) and freeze, stirring occasionally. Just before serving transfer to a blender and whizz to a slush. Or simply scrape with a fork to get mounds of granular frozen granita.

Granita di caffé
Coffee water ice

Coffee bars in the Campania region of Italy offer this delicious granita during the hot summer months, often topped with a dollop of whipped cream. It is a wonderful way to have coffee on a hot afternoon.

125 g sugar
2 tablespoons water
6 cups strong black coffee
2 teaspoons cocoa powder

Dissolve the sugar in the water in a pot and boil for several minutes to reduce it to a syrup. Pour the coffee into the syrup, mix in the cocoa.

Pour into a shallow tray (steel if you have it) and freeze, stirring occasionally. Just before serving transfer to a blender and whizz to a slush. Or scrape with a fork to create mounds of granular frozen granita.

Variation
Add ¹/₄ cup Grand Marnier to the mixture. Note that, with the addition of the liqueur, the mixture will not freeze as solidly.

Gelato
Ice cream

Use the ice cream base and mix it with whatever fruit purée you like to make different flavours. Gelato is creamier and more satisfying than granita. As a dessert it might be combined with a simple macaroon or served with a sprinkle of ground coffee and a drizzle of Grand Mariner. However you choose to serve it, keep it simple and don't try to overpower the flavour of the ice cream, which is beautiful by itself.

Ice cream base
3 egg yolks
1 cup sugar
³/₄ cup milk
600 ml cream

Beat the eggs and sugar, add the milk and heat in a double boiler over a low heat. Slowly add the cream, stirring occasionally until the mixture thickens. Pour into a metal dish or tray and freeze, stirring occasionally.

Fruit purée
You might like to add a dash of some liqueur, say 2 tablespoons, to jazz up a simple gelato. Some liqueurs go particularly well with certain fruits, for example Amaretto and apricots, strawberries and Grand Mariner.

4 cups fruit
juice of 1 lemon
¹/₃ cup sugar

Purée all 3 ingredients in a food processor. Stir into the ice cream base and put in the freezer, stirring every so often until frozen.

Zabaglione

A rich, creamy custard-like dessert, this is served warm as a topping over fruits and puddings or on its own in a glass. The only drawback is that you have to make zabaglione on the spot, which means 15–20 minutes of your time away from the guests. Try substituting a good port for the Marsala.

6 egg yolks
¹/₄ cup sugar
¹/₄ cup Marsala

Beat the egg yolks and sugar together. Heat in a double boiler, beating constantly until it thickens, then slowly add the liquid, still beating all the while. Pour into glasses and serve immediately. Or serve over fresh fruit such as strawberries or raspberries in season.

Soufflé di zabaglione
Zabaglione soufflé

This is a convenient variation when time is a problem but you want to have that creamy richness of zabaglione. You make this soufflé ahead of time (e.g. in the morning for that evening's dessert) and keep it in the refrigerator. It will, however, begin to separate if made too long in advance.

1 tablespoon gelatine
$^1/_3$ cup warm water
3 eggs, separated
$^2/_3$ cup sugar
$^1/_2$ cup Marsala or sweet sherry

Dissolve the gelatine in the water. Beat egg yolks and sugar together, beat in the gelatine, slowly beat in the Marsala. Place the mixture in a bowl over boiling water and continue mixing until it thickens.

Remove from the heat and cool. Beat the egg whites to stiff peaks and fold into the yolk mixture. Pour into serving glasses and chill.

Torta di fichi
Fig and nut cake

This is an exceptionally fine fruit cake with a chocolate difference.

125 g toasted hazelnuts
90 g slivered almonds
125 g dried figs
125 g mixed peel
90 g dark chocolate
3 eggs
$^1/_2$ cup sugar
1$^1/_4$ cups flour
1$^1/_2$ teaspoons baking powder

Pre-heat the oven to 190°C and grease a 20 x 10 cm loaf tin.

Roughly chop the nuts, figs, mixed peel and chocolate. Beat the eggs and sugar until light and fluffy. Stir the 2 mixtures together, sift in the flour and baking powder and mix until just blended. Spoon into the prepared tin and bake for 1 hour. Allow to cool slightly in the tin before turning out.

Frutti al liquore con fettuccine fritte
Liqueured fruit with deep-fried fettuccine

12 large strawberries
12 mandarin segments
2 tablespoons Grand Marnier
2 cups red wine
1 cup sugar
4 apples, peeled and cored
2 nectarines, peeled and pitted
18 grapes
oil
250 g fresh fettuccine
icing sugar
300 ml cream
1 teaspoon vanilla essence
1 tablespoon icing sugar

Put the strawberries and mandarin segments into a bowl, sprinkle with the Grand Marnier and allow to marinate for 4 hours.

Put the red wine and sugar into a pot and simmer to form a syrup, about 5 minutes. Slice each apple and nectarine into 8 pieces, add them to the pot and simmer about 2 minutes. Remove the pot from the heat and allow the fruits to cool in the liquid.

Just before serving, arrange the apples and nectarines in a circle on individual serving dishes. Place the mandarin segments and strawberries in the centre and top with grapes.

Heat the oil and deep-fry the fettuccine a few at a time for 1–2 seconds. Remove and dust liberally with icing sugar. Arrange in a lattice pattern over the fruit.

Whip the cream, vanilla and icing sugar to soft peaks and spoon a dollop next to the fruit. Serve at once.

Biscotti alle noccioline e cioccolata
Hazelnut and chocolate biscotti

Biscotti are biscuit-like rusks that go exceptionally well with coffee or wine.

$^3/_4$ cup hazelnuts
125 g butter
$^3/_4$ cup sugar
2 eggs
1 teaspoon vanilla essence
$^1/_4$ teaspoon almond essence
2 cups flour
$1^1/_2$ teaspoon baking powder
$^3/_4$ cup bitter-sweet chocolate, chopped

Pre-heat the oven to 180°C. Scatter the nuts in a baking pan and bake in the oven for 8-10 minutes, or until lightly toasted. Let cool 1 minute, rub between your fingers to remove the skins. Then chop the nuts coarsely.

Cream the butter and sugar together and beat in the eggs until smooth. Mix in the essences. Sift in the flour and baking powder and blend until well mixed, then stir in the chocolate and nuts.

Divide the dough in half and pat out into 2 logs about 15 mm high, 4 cm wide and 35 cm long on a greased and floured baking sheet. Leave at least 5 cm between the logs. Bake at 150°C for 20–25 minutes.

Let cool and then slice diagonally about 15 mm thick with a serrated knife. Place the slices on the baking sheet, well separated and bake a further 8–10 minutes. Allow to cool on a rack. Store in an airtight container.

Dolce alla sambucca
Sambucca cheesecake

1³/₄ cups ground almonds
¹/₄ cup sugar
60 g softened butter
³/₄ cup sugar
¹/₃ cup water
20 whole blanched almonds
2 cups ricotta cheese
¹/₄ cup sugar
2 tablespoons Sambucca
1 teaspoon vanilla
1 cup sour cream
3 tablespoons grated chocolate

Chocolate leaves
90 g dark chocolate
1 teaspoon butter
8–10 camellia or rose leaves

For the chocolate leaves, melt the chocolate and butter together and paint with a small brush over the underside of the leaves. Chill and then peel the leaves from the chocolate, starting from the stem end.

Butter a 23 cm springform tin. Mix the ground almonds, sugar and butter and press into the bottom of the prepared tin. Bake at 190°C for 10 minutes. Set aside to cool.

Caramelise the sugar and water. (Put the sugar and water in a pot and heat, stirring occasionally, until the mixture begins to turn brown.) Working quickly, dip the almonds in the caramelised sugar and place on a greased baking sheet to cool. Spread the remaining caramel over the crust; allow to cool so that the caramel sets hard.

Combine the ricotta, sugar, Sambucca, vanilla and sour cream in a food processor and whizz to a smooth consistency. Fold in the chocolate. Spread this mixture over the crust and freeze.

One hour before serving, remove the cake from the freezer and put into the fridge. Just before serving, remove the springform, decorate with the almonds and chocolate leaves and serve.

Dessert pizzas

Sure, why not? The idea of a yeast-based dessert is not new; almost every national cuisine has several examples of such sweet yeast cakes. One of the most traditional and best known sweet pizzas is the Schiacciata con l'uva or grape pizza. Made during grape harvest time, it is, for city dwellers, a living link with their rural roots. Sweet pizzas, like pizzas generally, should be eaten the day they are made.

Pizza dolce modesta
Modest dessert pizza

1 quantity yeast dough (see page 104)
250 g ricotta cheese
150 g cream cheese
1 tablespoon grated lemon rind
$^1/_2$ cup sugar

Lightly oil a 30 cm pizza pan and pre-heat the oven to 230°C.

Pull and push the dough into the pan. Cream the remaining ingredients together and spread over the base. Bake for 15-20 minutes.

Pizza alla frutta
Fruit pizza

250 g ricotta cheese
150 g cream cheese
$^1/_2$ cup sugar
1 tablespoon cinnamon
1 quantity yeast dough (see page 104)
2 apples, cored but not peeled, cut into rings
1 banana
$^1/_4$ cup fresh raspberries
$^1/_2$ cup raspberry jam
1 kiwifruit, sliced
1 tablespoon icing sugar

Lightly oil a 30 cm pizza pan and pre-heat the oven to 230°C.

Cream the ricotta, cream cheese, sugar and cinnamon together. Pull and push the dough into the pizza pan. Spoon dollops of the cheese mixture onto the base and press an apple ring onto each. Slice the banana and lay between the apple rings and bake for 15-20 minutes.

Remove from the oven and place a raspberry in the centre of each apple ring, spread the jam around the edge of the pizza and fit the kiwifruit in among the fruits. Dust lightly with the icing sugar and serve immediately.

Desserts

Schiacciata con l'uva
Grape pizza

1 quantity yeast dough (see page 104)
2 cups seedless grapes
$^1/_2$ cup icing sugar
1 teaspoon cinnamon
3 tablespoons sugar

Pre-heat the oven to 230°C.

Wash the grapes and remove the stalks. Shake off any excess water and, while they are still damp, toss them lightly in a bowl with the icing sugar and the cinnamon.

Pull and push the dough into a lightly oiled pizza pan or into a round on a baking sheet. Place the grapes decoratively on top of the base and sprinkle with sugar. Bake for 15–20 minutes. Remove from the oven and allow to cool for a few minutes before serving. Serve warm.

Tiramisu
Pick-me-up

Make this a day ahead and serve well chilled. Cream cheese may be substituted for mascarpone and sweet sherry for the Marsala. The traditional sponge fingers or savoiardi are often difficult to get and so use sponge cake instead.

1 cup Marsala
1 cup strong cold espresso coffee
2 x 23 cm sponge cakes or
  1 packet (about 24) sponge fingers
4 eggs, separated
3 tablespoons sugar
400 g mascarpone cheese

Lay 1 of the sponges or half of the sponge fingers in a serving dish slightly larger than the sponge. Mix half of the coffee with all the Marsala and sprinkle half of this mixture over the sponge.

Beat the egg yolks with half of the sugar and the remaining coffee, then add the mascarpone and mix to a smooth consistency. Beat the egg whites with the remaining sugar to stiff peaks and fold into the cheese mixture.

Spoon half of this mixture over the moistened sponge. Lay the remaining sponge or fingers on top of this and sprinkle with the remaining Marsala mixture, then spoon over the remaining cheese mixture.

Sprinkle with grated dark chocolate or ground coffee and refrigerate until required.

Colomba di Pasqua
Dove of Easter

This dove-shaped yeast cake is made and sold throughout Italy during Easter. There are many modern versions with different fillings and toppings but this is the easier, more traditional recipe. It is served after the main meal, with coffee.

Dough

2 tablespoons dry yeast
$^1/_4$ cup warm water
$^1/_2$ teaspoon sugar
$^1/_2$ cup warm milk
$^1/_2$ cup melted butter
$^1/_4$ cup sugar
2 tablespoons grated lemon rind
2 tablespoons vanilla essence
2 eggs
2 egg yolks
$4^1/_2$ cups flour

Marzipan

1 cup ground almonds
1 cup icing sugar
1 egg white
1 teaspoon lemon juice

Topping

1 cup slivered almonds
1 egg
sugar

Combine the yeast, warm water, sugar and warm milk in a plastic bowl. Leave 5–10 minutes to foam. Cream the melted butter, sugar, lemon rind and vanilla and beat in the eggs and egg yolks. Mix in the flour and the yeast mixture and knead to a smooth consistency. Put the dough back into the bowl, cover with a teatowel and let rise for about 1 hour.

Divide the dough in half and roll 1 piece into a long oblong. Place on a lightly oiled baking sheet. Roll the second piece into a long, thin triangle and place on top of the first, cross-wise. Twist the top triangle as shown to form the body of the bird.

Mix the marzipan ingredients together. Roll balls of marzipan and press into the wing tips as shown, cover with a teatowel and allow to rise for about 20 minutes. Brush with egg and sprinkle with sugar and almonds and bake at 150°C for 40–50 minutes, covering for the last 15 minutes if it is becoming too dark.

La zuppa inglese
Trifle

Zuppa inglese and tiramisu are often confused. They are similar in that they are sponge fingers (savoiardi in Italian) soaked in a liquid and covered in a rich mixture. The main difference is that zuppa inglese is a rum-flavoured trifle and tiramisu is flavoured with coffee and Marsala and includes a creamy mascarpone cheese in its ingredients. Here I give you a very rich zuppa inglese recipe and the tiramisu recipe back on page 121 so you may make them both and realise the subtle and delicious differences between them. Sometimes zuppa inglese is topped with whipped cream and not baked. Either way it should be served chilled.

1 egg
3 egg yolks
¼ cup sugar
1 tablespoon cornflour
600 ml cream
3 egg whites
2 tablespoons icing sugar
1 packet savoiardi or 2 x 21 cm sponge cakes
½ cup rum
¼ cup liqueur (of your choice)
¼ cup grated lemon rind or candied peel

Make the custard by beating the egg, egg yolks, sugar and cornflour together. Warm the cream and add a little to the egg mixture, stirring constantly and then slowly stirring in the remaining cream. Cook over a gentle heat, stirring often until the custard thickens. Be sure to stir well so that the custard doesn't stick to the bottom of the pan. Remove from the heat and allow to cool.

Beat the egg whites and icing sugar together to stiff peaks and set aside until required.

Either layer with the savoiardi or use the sponge cakes as described.

Cut the bottom third from each sponge cake so that you have 2 thick sponge cakes and 2 thin sponge cakes in 21 cm rounds.

Place the 2 thin rounds on top of each other in a baking dish just a little larger than the rounds (about 23 cm diameter) and sprinkle with half of the rum. Spread a third of the custard over the rum-soaked cake and place 1 of the remaining cake rounds on that and sprinkle with the liqueur. Spoon on a third of the custard, then scatter with the mixed peel. Place the last round of cake on that and sprinkle with the remaining rum.

Spread with the remaining custard and top with the beaten egg whites, bringing them right out to the edge of the dish. Bake for 20 minutes at 140°C. Allow to cool completely before serving.

In fact, this is really best made the day before you serve it since the flavours need to mingle together for a while.

La bonissima
Walnut and honey pie

Pastry
1¹/₂ cups flour
¹/₄ cup caster sugar
150 g butter
1 egg yolk
1 egg
1 tablespoon milk

Put the ingredients into a food processor and whizz. Tip out and knead to a smooth dough. Cover and let rest while you make the filling.

Filling
2¹/₂ cups walnuts
1 cup honey
1 lemon rind, grated
¹/₄ cup Marsala
¹/₄ cup dried breadcrumbs
2 tablespoons sugar
1 egg yolk

Blanch the walnuts and rub off the skin, if you can be bothered. Chop coarsely.

Heat the honey, walnuts and lemon rind together in a pot until all the nuts are coated with honey. Remove from the heat and stir in the Marsala and leave to cool.

Pre-heat the oven to 180°C. Lightly oil and flour a 20 cm springform pan.

Roll out two-thirds of the dough and line the bottom and sides of the pan. Sprinkle the breadcrumbs and sugar over the bottom and add the filling. Cover with the remaining dough, which has been rolled out to fit. Prick all over with a fork and brush with beaten egg yolk. Or make a lattice topping.

Bake for 25–30 minutes or until the pastry is golden brown. Allow to cool in the tin then transfer to a decorative plate to serve.

This can be made up to 2 days in advance.

Panettone
Italian Christmas bread

Panettone is a yeast bread somewhat like a French brioche, but with a few raisins and spices added. It originated in Milan, which is still the home of the world's best panettone. This recipe, though, will provide you with a very reasonable and comparatively easy version of that famous cake/bread. It should be made a day before it is eaten as it requires that time for the flavour and texture to develop properly. It is delicious sliced (perhaps lightly toasted first) and spread with butter and goes particularly well with freshly brewed coffee.

Dough
1/2 **cup raisins**
1/4 **cup mixed peel**
1/2 **cup sweet sherry**
1 1/2 **tablespoons dry active yeast**
1 **teaspoon sugar**
1/4 **cup warm water**
1/2 **cup milk**
90 g **butter**
1 **tablespoon grated lemon rind**
1 **cup sugar**
2 **teaspoons vanilla essence**
4 **cups flour**
3 **eggs**
25 g **melted butter**

Pre-heat the oven to 200°C. Lightly oil and line with baking paper a high-sided cylindrical tin about 14 cm in diameter and 18 cm high.

Put the raisins, mixed peel and sherry in a small bowl and leave for 30 minutes.

Put the yeast, 1 teaspoon of sugar and warm water in a small plastic bowl and leave for 5 minutes to activate.

Heat the milk and butter together until the butter has melted. Add the grated lemon rind, cup of sugar and vanilla and stir together.

Add the flour and eggs to the milk mixture, along with the yeast mixture. Mix well with a wooden spoon. Add the raisins, mixed peel and whatever liquid hasn't been absorbed by the fruit to the dough and mix well. The dough will be sloppy at this stage. Cover with a teatowel and leave to rise in a warm (not hot) place for about 2 hours.

Scatter some flour onto the benchtop and scrape the dough onto it. Sprinkle with a little flour and knead for a few minutes. Shape into a ball and place in the prepared baking dish. Cover and leave in a warm place to rise for 1 hour.

Brush the melted butter over the top of the panettone, then bake for 15 minutes at 200°C. Reduce the heat to 180°C and bake a further 35–40 minutes until a knife inserted in the centre comes out cleanly and the panettone sounds hollow when tapped. If the top begins to brown too much before the inside is baked then cover it with some foil and continue baking. Allow the panettone to cool in the tin. Panettone will keep as long as any other fresh bread.

Desserts

Crostoli

These light, rather plain biscuits, which go well with coffee, are made from a sweetened pasta dough cut into diamond shapes and deep-fried.

1 cup flour
2 tablespoons icing sugar
1 teaspoon cinnamon
1 egg
1 egg yolk
2 tablespoons cream

Whizz all the ingredients in a food processor and roll into sheets as you would for pasta. Cut the sheets into wide strips with a pastry-cutter and then cut the strips into diamonds.

Deep-fry briefly, turning once until the dough is cooked, about 30 seconds. Remove, drain on absorbent paper and dust with icing sugar while they are still hot.

Panforte

This delicious Italian chocolate nougat-like cake is served in thin wedges with coffee. It keeps well.

1 cup whole hazelnuts
1 cup slivered almonds
$^1/_3$ cup glacé cherries
$^1/_3$ cup glacé pawpaw
$^1/_3$ cup dried apricots
$^1/_3$ cup candied peel
2 tablespoons cocoa
1 cup flour
$^1/_2$ cup sugar
$^1/_2$ cup liquid honey
$^1/_3$ cup dark chocolate

Pre-heat the oven to 160°C.

Put the hazelnuts, almonds, cherries, pawpaw, apricots, peel, cocoa and flour into a bowl and mix well together.

Put the sugar and honey into a pot and bring to the boil, stirring until the sugar is dissolved. Add the chocolate and stir until it is all melted. Pour this mixture over the nut mixture and mix well.

Rub some butter onto the palms of your hands, tip the dough onto a buttered benchtop and knead together. Press the dough into a 21 cm non-stick pan and bake for 30 minutes.

Allow to cool in the container. Store wrapped in foil. To serve cut into small wedges.

Index

Index

Index

Index

Index